T0303364

Blue

Blue

A ST. BARTS MEMOIR

DAVID COGGINS

pH powerHouse Books Brooklyn, NY

To Wendy, David, and Sarah

Blue

CONTENTS

PREFACE

For many who live in the north to head south in late winter is a matter of survival. To feel the heat of tropical sun, to swim in the blue sea is to be reborn. Trading brown city for green hills, icy sidewalk for sandy beach gives you reason to keep on living.

My family's place in the sun is the island of Saint Barthélemy in the French West Indies. When we first started going in the mid-1990s, we traveled together. Now the four of us arrive separately from our respective homes in the U.S. It takes some effort to get there—two, usually three flights. When the little commuter plane touches down on the narrow airstrip and comes to a stop short of the beach, the feeling is one of relief and delight.

Though more houses dot the hills now and roads are busier, St. Barts retains its beauty and charm. This book is a testament to our long-standing affection—over 20 years now—for this beatific Caribbean sanctuary. It's an attempt to

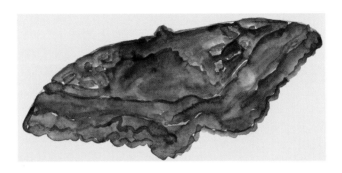

capture in words and pictures the spirit of the place, which, I'm afraid, is a little like trying to net a butterfly.

It takes a day or two to get into the rhythm. You go for a swim, get a little color, have a bit of rum. Gears start to shift. You feel a sense of freedom, of ease. You feel a little giddy. We take pleasure in our simple island rituals: feeding tortoises in the villa garden, swimming at Gouverneur beach, outdoor lunches overlooking the sea. Hikes on the bluffs, hours of reading, drinks with friends.

The villa we rent has a gazebo where I go in the morning to draw and read. One or two doves join me, shyly waiting for bits of dry baguette. At first I am occupied with sketchbook and watercolors, but after a while the goats show up. They scramble along the hillside 30 yards away. Then the sugarbirds come, and the hummingbirds. They hover over the flowers around the pool. Below a sailboat appears suddenly from behind the bluff and slides in and out of the waves.

Tropicbirds with their long elegant tails circle the rocky shoreline. My gaze goes to the horizon, where the blue sea meets the blue sky. Slip for a few minutes into reverie. There is a splash, a familiar face surfaces at the side of the pool and smiles.

For all those who have places in the sun, or dream of places in the sun, I hope this book, should it find its way to you, strikes a warm chord.

David Coggins
Winter 2018

St. Barts
from above

ONE

The villa sits on the side of a cliff.

We drive up a mountain then down a dirt road that seems to end in air. We get out of the Moke. Across a valley, mountains run bumpy as a dinosaur's back between bowls of cobalt-blue sea. White clouds drift in an azure sky. Small islands punctuate the horizon. The air is fresh. You want to burst out in song. Instead, we stand mute.

"*Bienvenue à St. Barth.*" A barefooted woman in cutoffs holds out her hand. On her hip is a small child. "*Je m'appelle Ana. Ceçi est Lucas.*" Ana has bright eyes and a brilliant smile. Her hair is a crown of ebony curls. She picks up the baby's hand and waves it. Wendy takes his finger. The boy also has a crown of curls. He smiles then buries his face in his mother's breast. "*Je suis la femme de chambre,*" Ana says.

She leads us upstairs to the house. On a table is a spray of pink bougainvillea. "Did you put the flowers here?" Wendy asks Ana. "They're beautiful."

"*Je suis brésilien,*" Ana says. "*Je ne parle pas anglais.*"

"*Les fleurs sont beaux. Merci beaucoup.*"

"Can I hold him?" Sarah asks. She takes Lucas in her arms. He stares at her. "His eyes are so big and brown. It's O.K., Lucas, I'm your friend."

I step out onto the terrace. Breeze like a gentle hand. Small birds dip in and out of the shell of an old coconut filled with sugar. I close my eyes, feel the sun on my face. David joins me.

"A hundred and eighty degrees," I say. "The view."

"There's a bottle of Champagne in the refrigerator."

It's February 1994.

Saint Barthelémy's 10 square miles is home to less than 10,000 residents. Seven miles around, it takes less than an hour to circle the island. There are no golf courses, no casinos, and, so it's said, no buildings taller than a palm tree. There are three ways to get here by sea: private boat, public ferry, or cruise ship.

Many people, if not most, take a small commercial

plane from St. Martin and hold on for dear life as the
plane drops sharply between two steep hills. It lands on an
unnervingly short runway that ends within steps of a beach.
In the early days, a car was driven back and forth signaling
that it was safe to land. People like to take photos from the
hilltop roundabout as the plane swoops down like a clunky
bird of prey.

I drive with Wendy down the mountain to Gustavia.
The road is narrow and winding. The morning sea glimmers
between hills like a necklace of blue diamonds. In the
grocery store are magnums of Champagne, quail eggs,
melons from Guadeloupe, clumps of mache, butter from
Brittany, and shelves of bottled water.

On Rue du Général de Gaulle, store shutters are open,
people sit with coffee and cigarettes at café tables. Short-
legged mutts stride around like mayors. Among the modern
shops are old Creole houses made of wood with porches
of frilly trim. Scooters and small cars jockey in the narrow
streets. "Not a bad little town."

"Completely charming," Wendy says.

We walk along the harbor past yachts tied to the quay and farther out swaying sailboats. Heavy ropes creak as they tug at the steel cleats. Small boats motor slowly toward open water. Up the green hills from the harbor are the remains of stone forts and a still functioning lighthouse. We stop at a *boulangerie* and buy bread and cheese, salads, and wine.

A sign in the villa tells us to conserve water. The roof of the house is made of corrugated metal that funnels rainwater through gutters to cisterns beneath the house.

The house is too isolated to be connected to the island's water supply. When rain is scarce, water is delivered for a price in a big truck.

The tiny pool is full of clean water. Around it are bushes alive with flowers and bees, lizards and butterflies. And at this moment in time four blinking, dazzled northerners. I look down at my baggy trunks. I feel a little silly smearing thick white cream on my forehead.

Gouverneur

"You have to rub it in, Dad. You can't just glop it on."

"Dad thinks it's war paint," David says.

Wendy and Sarah are sun worshippers. They have an array of lotions and take to the tiles like seals. They want to trade Nordic pale for tropic bronze. David has never had a tan. He burns. He protects his fair skin by reading on the veranda by the pool and staying out of the sun.

I sit down in a plastic chair, half under a small palm tree. I wouldn't mind a little color, but what I really need is to feel the heat. Like a big steak from the freezer, I need to thaw. I open Alexander Theroux's book, *The Primary Colors.* In the essay about blue, he writes that Paul Bowles describes the sea off the coast of Tangier as "peacock feather blue." I get up and walk to the hillside. I look out at the valley and the mountains and the sea. I spread my arms and yell, "YES!"

The small *anse*, or cove, of Gouverneur has a lovely beach protected by hills of rock and cactus. Wild goats tear at patches of green, elegant tropicbirds with long white tails loop back and forth. Sailboats and yachts pass like props in the distance. Gangs of jet skis occasionally blight the horizon. Behind the beach is a large private estate.

Walking into the sea is primeval and profound. You feel like the animal you are. You dive in, swim out. It's a little chilly at first then fine. The waves are gentle. You turn over on your back and spit out salt water. The sun is high in the sky. You dive, resurface, shake your head. The steak is thawed. "Let's walk to the end of the beach."

A few kids body surf, young couples doze on towels. A topless woman leans back on her arms and stares out dreamily. Near the end of the bay, three nude men chat as if at a backyard barbecue. They are brown as beavers.

"It's a French island," Wendy says.

"Did you say flesh island?"

The sea is the ultimate democracy, the ultimate fact. It accepts all, it is all. Birth, death, beauty, violence, peace, tragedy. It is the Sirens, Magellan, Melville, Cousteau. Santa Maria, Titanic, Spray, U-2 boat. It is dolphin, shark, coral. It is music, pleasure, infinity. It is blue, the truest thing we know. A child always colors the sea blue. The earth will be sea again one day.

Sunset. The wind, stronger up here than down in the valley, is dying down. We open a bottle of Champagne. Clouds move spritely across the pink and blue sky. We sit on the terrace and watch cars and trucks negotiate the road below. "I can't believe the main road is no wider than a driveway." A car stops and backs up to let another car pass.

A sliver of moon appears, stars. "You're already red," I say to Sarah.

"Pink. Salmon pink. I love it here."

"So quiet."

"Peaceful."

Lights shine in the houses on the hills. A road spirals upward into the darkening sky.

"I hope the restaurants are as good as they say they are," David says.

"Time to find out," I say and down the mountain we go.

We sit at a table facing the inky water of the outer harbor where sailboats and cruise ships are anchored. The light in the distant lighthouse flashes green. Tables are full. A cat slinks about. There's a California freshness to the place. "We're eating between the sea and a cemetery," I say.

One of the men at the boisterous table next to us just sold his business. *"Beaucoup, beaucoup,"* the French waiter says and rubs his thumb over his fingers.

"Let me guess. The one smoking the foot-long cigar?"

Forks clash over the slice of coconut tart on our table. "Have some of my passion fruit sorbet."

"This is shrub." The waiter sets down four small glasses of opaque liquid at the end of the meal. "It's a recipe from Maya's mother. Rum with spices."

Maya appears, smiling, her hands in the pockets of her chef's apron. "I love your hair," she says to Wendy.

"I love your food. This is our first time here."

"Welcome to the island. Are you renting a villa?"

"Yes, in Lurin."

"The quiet side. That's where we live."

"What does shrub mean?"

"Shrub means witch's brew in Creole." A thin, grinning man is at the table, Maya's husband Randy. Scholar's glasses sit on the prow of his nose. "I grew up on Nantucket. Maya grew up on Guadeloupe. I sailed down here years ago. We met and opened a restaurant. We lived on my sailboat."

"Did you know what you were doing?"

"Are you kidding?" Randy runs his hand through his thick sandy hair. "I was a sailor and did carpentry. It was a good thing Maya knew how to cook."

Tiny ants swarm over the dead grasshopper in my paint box. Two dragonflies joined end to end flit by, air mates. I'm making a drawing of Wendy in small dots of watercolor on gridded paper.

"Seurat meets Chuck Close," David says. He swims laps in the wee pool, five strokes to a lap. "Hard to get a workout."

"Did you know that Jane Austen died when she was 41?"

A hawk hovers then plunges into the valley. "Did you know that James Bond wrote a guide to the birds of the West Indies?"

"007?"

"James Bond was an ornithologist. Ian Fleming copped his name and used it for his spy."

"Ana calls the yellow and black birds at the coconut feeder *les sucriers*. The sugarbirds. They have curved beaks that get deep into flowers."

"Who needs flowers? They've got a coconut full of sugar."

"Look, there's a black hummingbird! It has a green crest."

"More like a mohawk," Sarah says.

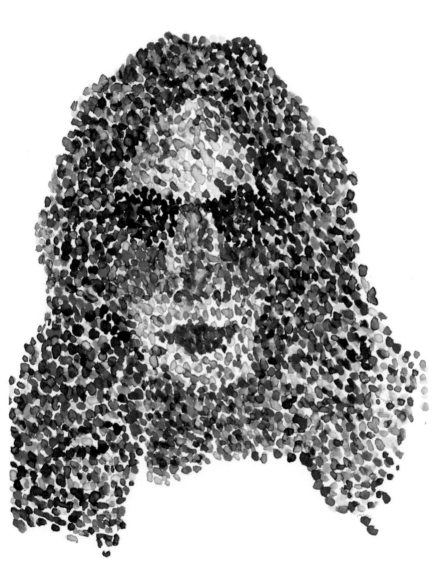

A young man, thin and tan in khaki shorts and boots, trims the bushes and rakes the ground of every fallen leaf, shriveled flower, and dead insect. The villa's gardens are clean as Maya's tablecloths. He waters pots and struggling plants. He gazes for a while at the panoramic view and then vanishes down the hill in a rusty truck. Minutes later the wind starts spreading another layer of leaves and flowers on the immaculate soil.

The gardens on the mountainside have little protection against the wind. Bougainvillea and oleander grow but don't thrive. Hibiscus and allamanda blossoms cling to spindly bushes. What the gardens lack in lushness, the view makes up for in splendor.

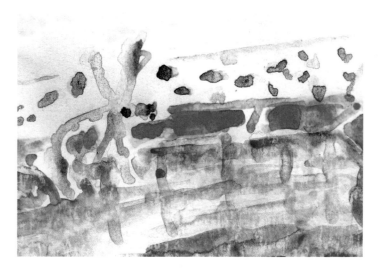

Hand-laid walls of weathered coral crisscross the hills of sunburnt grass. There are houses but no crops in the barren fields that rise up from the sea. In yards by the road, tamarind trees with craggy trunks, big around as a young whale, fan out over goats and chickens, bougainvillea and hibiscus.

This is the *côte sauvage*, the wild side of the island. You have to cross Morne de Grand Fond to get here. (*Morne* is small mountain in French.) When you come down the mountain through the valley you are at the Atlantic. The wind is strong, waves crash.

The narrow road runs by the sea. We walk along the rocky beach for a while looking out at the panorama of sky and sea. Three thousand miles away is Africa.

The coral for the walls was gathered from the beach long ago, probably when the road was a footpath; the stones were laid simply one on top of the other. The modest houses here belong to islanders. There are no hotels, few villas. Nureyev built a house on this side of the island. Not much more than a fisherman's hut, it sits on an outcrop of rock just off the road. There on a deck he danced, it is said, to the furious music of the ocean.

On one side of the path is a mass of wild green, on the other a scruffy field where two or three cows graze with resignation. Small lizards scuttle in the hot sand. Wendy picks a flower hanging from a bush. The sweet heavy smell reminds me of my grandmother. We pass through dunes.

The long beach is covered with shells, coral, stones of all shapes and sizes. Plus washed up bits of human detritus: bottles, pieces of sodden wood, plastic rope. It's almost deserted. We crunch along slowly, trying to avoid the eddying pools. Waves when they recede crackle over the rocks. A French couple collects sea urchins at the bottom of the high bluff at the end of the beach.

"These rocks are amazing. Look at this one, it's beautiful. And this one. It's a perfect oval." Wendy gathers shells then finds a sandy spot to stretch out. I keep scrambling, picking up, examining, comparing rock after

Chevreau

Colombier Flamands

Corossol

Public

S. T.

La Pain
de Sucre

Gustavia

Saint
Barthélemy

Tortue
Pointe Milou
Mont Jean
Lorient
Vitet
Grand Fond
saline
Gouverneur

rock. Pockets and hands full, I stumble back. My tennis shoes are soaked.

"What are you going to do with them?"

"I'm keeping the best, a few of the best."

"Best?"

"Yes, these dark gray ones that are round and smooth as eggs. It's taken millions and millions of years…"

"But what are you going do with them?"

"I don't know. Pile them up, put them around."

"They're heavy. You have lots of them. Not going to take them back, are you?"

"I like rocks."

"You should like something lighter."

At the beach today, I read in Aldo Buzzi's *Journey to the Land of the Flies* about Verdi's trip to St. Petersburg for the premiere of his opera, *La Forza del Destino.* Verdi liked to dine well and brought with him hundreds of bottles of French wine and Champagne. No need to do that here. The wine shops and restaurants runneth over with excellent wines and Champagnes all freighted across the ocean. It's shocking to think about the quality and quantity of the stuff brought to this dot on the map, thousands of miles from the vineyards and cellars of France. And not only wine. Aside from bread and some fish, fruit, and vegetables, all food is imported.

St. Barts was once Swedish. Louis XVI traded the island, like Park Place or more like Marvin Gardens, in the late 18th century for the right to sell goods in Sweden. A hundred years later, it came back to France. Gustavia, the main port, still has its Swedish name as do some streets and buildings. Rue du Roi Oscar II runs parallel to Rue du General de Gaulle on the north side of town. Rue Samuel Fahlberg (named after a Swedish administrator and cartographer) intersects with Rue Victor Hugo.

Saint Barthelémy was named by one of Europe's early restless souls. Christoforo Colombo came upon the island in 1493 and named it after his brother, Bartoloméo. The Caribs and the Arawak, Amerindian tribes that predated European settlement, called it Ouanalao, believed to be their word for pelican.

The island was under Spanish
and English rule for a while. Small
and lacking in resources, subject
to hurricanes and droughts, no
European empire really cared about
it until the French-Dutch adventurer
Rémy de Haenen landed his two-
seater plane, Cucaracha, on a field
here in 1945. With time, it opened
to the world's pleasure seekers; this
poor dry rock became a place in the
20th century for the well-off to relax
or to party. Petiteness and paucity of
arable soil kept away big planes and
big development but not in the end
big spenders.

Coming back from town
one morning, Wendy and I meet
Monsieur Lassus, the owner of the
villa. He and Ana are on the side of
the mountain that looks down at
the airport and the pond. Monsieur
Lassus is short and stocky with thick
white hair. A widower, he lives in a
small house behind the villa. He tells
us Hurricane Luis was one of the
worst ever to hit the island. *"Beaucoup
de damage. Le cyclone l'année dernière. Très,
très fort. . ."*

"*Tous les toits,*" Ana says. She throws
her arms up. "*Disparu.* Bye-bye."

A German shepherd, pink tongue dangling, lopes by a beautiful actress lying on the beach. A man follows the woman into the water. He paddles about closer than propriety would allow, considering that she doesn't know him. Not only that, he is "naked as a jaybird," as my mother used to say.

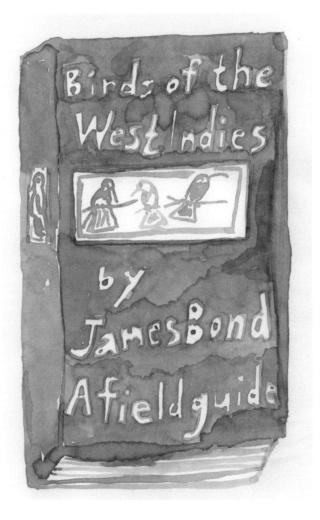

TWO

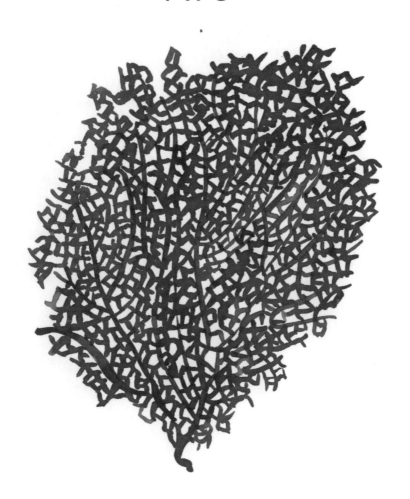

This year we are staying not at the top of the mountain but down below by the water.

Our yellow house has blue shutters and a plastic picket fence that encloses a patchy yard where lizards sun. Through the gate and across 30 feet of sand is the sea. Birds swoop among small boats moored just offshore. Women on their lunch break shed their clothes in piles on the beach and breaststroke through the lapping waves. Wendy and Sarah set salads and cheeses on the outdoor table. Wine is poured. "Here's to Freddy," Sarah says.

"Who's Freddy?"

"Freddy Alfresco. He always eats outside."

"Would you like some *salade de supions?* Little squids."

"The sound of waves is such a natural thing," I say. "It's a pity you have to go so far to hear it."

The town, not a town really but a neighborhood, is called Lorient. The school and the grocery store are on the main island road, a short walk from the house. Nearby are the library and the church. "Did you see the little joint by the grocery store? It's called Jojo Burger."

"You mean *Zjho zjho Bear-gair?*" Sarah says.

The island is a place to read, the sun a lamp, the beach a big bed. Wendy devours three books in a week. She keeps a running list of titles. Now it's *Andorra* by Peter Cameron. Sarah is reading *My Russian Love*. David, a junior in college, is reading *Crime and Punishment*. One morning on the way to Gustavia in the Jeep he goes into great detail about the murder. "You're the only person on the island reading Dostoyevsky."

"I'm sure lots of people are reading murder mysteries."

We pass the airport as a plane shimmies between the hills and bounces lightly on the runway. After the roundabout, the road, barely two lanes wide, snakes down through the "industrial" section of town, past stores that sell hammers and saws, dishware, and outdoor furniture. A huge cargo boat is tied up at the pier. After passing the giant rock at the water's edge, we enter the harbor. Right before the ferry landing, traffic stops.

"Not a traffic jam! Not on the island, not in paradise!"

"No murderous rages, Dad."

Taxi vans wheedle out of a parking lot onto the main road, carrying daytrippers from cruise ships. As we inch along, we see couple after couple—human flowers of pink, yellow, and green—stepping gingerly from dinghies.

At La Rotisserie, we buy roasted chicken, two or three salads, and *une tarte au citron.* Wendy chats with Eveline, the woman who works behind the counter. *"Vous avez passé une bonne année?"* Eveline asks. She hands Wendy cartons wrapped in foil.

    "Oui, une bonne année. Et vous?"

    "Moi aussi."

    "Merci beaucoup."

    "Mon plaisir. Bonne journée."

    "Bonne journée à vous. Au revoir."

Sarah and I hike up to the Catholic church. In the wall are conch shells containing holy water. There's a neon star and a braying lamb in stained glass. In the Lorient cemetery, bright white markers in stone and wood stand by garish plastic flowers. On some, the names of the dead have been written by hand. *Ici Reposent M. et Mme Charles Rudin.* No dates. People have been living here for centuries. Born on the island, buried on the island. True of most of them, I think.

The green shutters of the library are folded back. Inside the front door is a big stack of *National Geographic* magazines. Shelves of books line the walls of an inviting, intimate room. "Too bad no one is in the library."

"Dad, this is an island. The sun is shining."

Outside the grocery store are hundreds of crushed, rusty caps from bottles of Heineken and Carib beer. The school playground, just off the main road, is full of noisy, happy children. A mural of a snowy winter scene is painted on the wall of the school.

"When are they in class? Every time we go by, the kids are outside playing."

"It's an island, Sarah. The sun is..."

"Right. Let's hit the beach."

We travel across the island to La Langouste, a modest restaurant in the Baie des Anges Hotel overlooking Flamands beach. Its specialty is *langouste,* the spiny lobster that thrives in Caribbean waters. An islander recommended the place. *"La langouste n'a pas de griffes...de pinces.* They pull from the tank and hold by their long antennae to show you."

We drive down a long winding road. While we wait to be seated, I see that the *langouste* tank is empty. A matronly woman greets us politely and leads us to a table. As she hands us our menus, she says, "We have no *langouste* tonight. *Je suis desolée.*"

In the garden bar of Le Tamarin is a tamarind tree of considerable girth. Sitting beneath its vast canopy, next to its rugged bark, you are in the presence of strength and age, secure as a child in her father's lap. Lights are strung through the tree's branches. A large caged parrot casts a bulbous eye in our direction. The roof of the open-air restaurant is supported by giant Indonesian joists and columns, wonderfully carved and aged.

We eat wahoo and daurade, local fish. Plastic curtains are lowered for a five-minute spray of rain. We have *rhum vanille.* Sarah wanders in the garden. David lights a cigar. The waiter tells us that people on the *côte sauvage* built their houses next to

la langouste

tamarind trees. "To protect them from *le cyclone*."

We drive up the dark mountain. Outside the villa, we look for the comet. The black sky bristles with stars. We have been following the progression of Comet Hyakutake the last several nights. We can't see it moving, but the tail is visible as a white blur to the naked eye and is in a different spot each night. It's in the eastern sky moving northwesterly. We orient it on the bright star Arcturus.

"There it is."

"The man who first saw it was Japanese. Just a couple of months ago. It's named after him. He's an amateur, saw it through binoculars."

"Can you see it in the city?"

"No, you've got to be where the air is clear and not affected by urban lights."

"Like on a mountain on an island in the Caribbean," David says.

"*Par exemple.*"

St. Barts has glamour, it's true. It also has wild goats. You might see a movie star or two, but even better you might meet Jean-Pierre Ballagny. Jean-Pierre, a native of France, is a painter. Divorced, a father of three daughters, he left France some years ago for Africa. He was sick and thought he had a short time to live. Time passed, death came not, so he got on a catamaran as a novice sailor and crossed the Atlantic to Brazil. On St. Barts, he worked as a carpenter and took up painting. He married Bernadette from Biarritz.

Not a tall man, Jean-Pierre is larger than life. He is handsome, a bit roguish, and has shaggy white hair set off by a deep tan and nicotine-stained teeth. He has a quick smile and charm to burn. One morning we visit his studio in

Corossol. It's a shack, literally, but filled with his paintings, pots of brushes, books, and Ecuadorian textiles, it's a very stylish shack.

He serves us coffee in the villa he's renting up the hill from the studio. We sit on a porch that wraps around the pink wooden house. Separate bedroom bungalows surround a tiny pool. The whole place is overrun with entwined boughs of jasmine, bushes of hibiscus, and cats. Jean-Pierre loves cats.

"The house was filled with butterflies after *le cyclone*."

"That sounds lovely."

"Yes, it was, but *le caca des papillons était tous le monde. Tous le monde caca.*"

He talks of moving to Costa Rica, "where the trees are full of parrots and monkeys eating mangoes. I wouldn't move back to Paris. It's cold. People are sad."

Back in town, we stop at the wine shop. "Do you like rosé?" Olivier, the young proprietor, asks. "People drink a lot of rosé here. Like Provence. It's a perfect wine for a hot place."

After a week, we move to Villa Lassus. I think I prefer a house with a view of the sea from on high rather than a house by the shore. Monsieur Lassus thanks Wendy for her letter, which has just arrived now, late February. He shows Wendy the U.S. postmark dated January 6th.

At Human Steps, a store in Gustavia, Wendy models a new slipper in front of a mirror. *"C'est très belle,"* the coquettish shop girl says. *"C'est trés élégante, très chic.* And very comfortable, yes?"

At La Rotisserie we buy a box of thin pretzel sticks dipped in chocolate. We can't resist the French description: *enrobé au chocolat.* Eveline puts the box in a black and white Fauchon bag along with our goat cheese and *pâté* and *céleri rémoulade.*

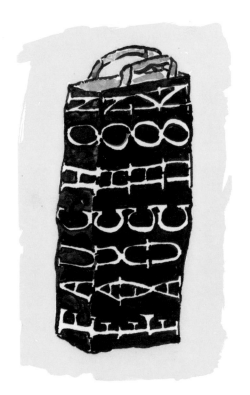

Shadows play on the tiles. A lizard poses on the stone wall, its orange dewlap opening and closing. I read that male lizards do this to attract females. No females are around at the moment, but there is a large grasshopper. The lizard nabs it and awkwardly but avidly works it down his throat. He comes down the wall and drinks water from a trough of grout. Quite civilized.

The view from my chair is of house, mountain, sea, endless sky. I brush a rough approximation of it into my sketchbook. A hawk is perched on the roof of the house, A bit offshore to the south is Île Coco. Occasionally, a small white plane descends through the valley.

The breeze picks up, flipping my page of wet watercolor. David's cap flies into the allamanda. The villa is on the windward (*au vent*) side of the island. The wind always blows on this side, gently at times, briskly at others. Sarah and Wendy are engrossed in books. After a dip in the pool, we have lunch on the verandah overlooking the sea.

"Would you want to have a house here?" I ask.

"Yes."

"Yes."

"Yes."

"Three yeses."

"Four."

At Gouverneur one afternoon, a French man and woman have lunch on the beach. They eat *langouste* at an elegantly set table. They sunbathe, drop towels over the chairs, and walk away. They step lightly as dancers in the smooth sand. They are the same height and have matching tans. Half an hour later, a man in white shorts and shirt gathers up the table and empty bottles.

An elderly American couple, beetle brown, roll in the surf. Waves knock them down. They get up, fall down, laugh, and roll. He has a small white goatee and a withered arm. She is plump and bethonged.

Man wearing
a watch

From *The Country of Marriage*: "...how deeply nostalgia
rules our lives after a point, nearly every act a beckoning
after an earlier, somehow purer act."

Drinks with Ben and Nancy, friends from home, at
their villa on the other side of the island, the leeward side.
The house is open to the air and has a view of the green hills
of St. Jean and Lorient.

Over dinner in Gustavia, we talk about youth – our
children, Ben's; marriage – Ben's and Nancy's soon to come;
death – Nancy's father; birth – my father's 75th birthday; life
– living on St. Barts.

We lift glasses. "Here's to your marriage."

"Here's to friendship."

"Here's to our fathers."

"Here's to *moules frites.*"

"By the sea."

"By the sea, by the sea," I sing. "By the beautiful sea."

"You and I, you and I," Nancy joins in. "Oh, how happy
we'll be."

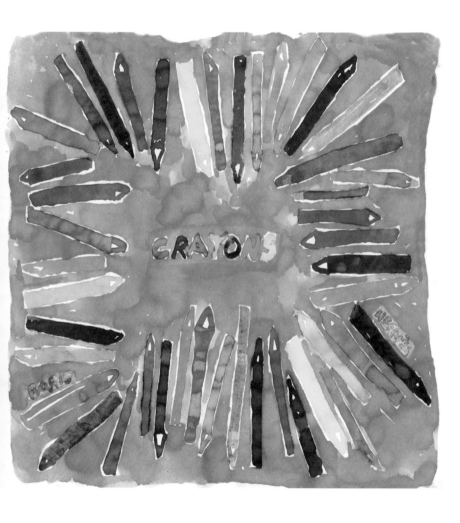

"I have to go find the money," the woman says in American English to the slim suited man. She lays the bright patterned scarf on the glass counter and adjusts her straw hat. "He's waiting outside. I'll be right back."

"Of course, Madame."

We look at the fancy shoes and leather notebooks. I glance out the window. "The pink ones are coming. From the ships. We should go. They'll be all over this place."

"Why don't you wait outside?"

A few minutes later, the woman in the straw hat comes out of the store followed by Wendy. Both are carrying the tell-tale bag.

"I thought you didn't like the scarves."

"It's for you."

"Wow, my very first Hermès scarf!"

"It's a pocket square. Covered in colored pencils, or *crayons* as the French call them. Perfect for an artist."

"Thank you."

"Just don't use it to clean your brushes.

the purple cow

THREE

sarah by the pool

Sarah steps down from the little plane and waves to us.

"You look marvelous." Wendy gives her a big hug.

"I've been working out." Sarah flexes her arm. She's 19, on spring break.

"Do I still have to carry your bag?"

"*Bonsoir,*" the bartender says.

"*Trois coupes de Champagne, s'il vous plaît.*"

"*Blanc ou rosé?*"

"You're wearing your little black dress," Sarah says to Wendy. "And you're brown already. You look marvelous." We are at Carl Gustav.

Friends serenade the bartender who is celebrating his 30th birthday. They dance to the Englishman playing the piano who sounds vaguely like Sting and looks vaguely like Jeff Bridges. We move to a table overlooking the harbor and, after ordering a nice wine, are told by the sommelier, "If you don't like, I will drink."

A group of raucous Texans enters the bar and orders colorful drinks. Soon they are doing the Macarena. Two chic Russian women sit down near the piano player. He can barely contain himself and starts crooning madly. The more made-up, more indomitable of the two women orders Champagne. With the usual ceremony, the bottle is opened and a small amount is poured into the flute. The woman sniffs, then throws it back as if it were a shot of vodka. She looks at the bottle cradled tenderly in the hands of the sommelier.

"This is not what I order," she says.

"Ah, bah oui, madame. Veuve Clicquot millisemé 1990."

"It is not, *monsieur*. I will not drink."

At tables near us are a bronzed gay couple and a rather dour American family. The teenage boy and girl frown at their menus. Their proper father speaks flawless French. Meanwhile the crowd at the bar is getting rowdier. As waiters arrive with our sashimi, the hotel receptionist is tossed fully clothed into the pool.

Butterflies, as if released from a jar, flit among the flowers, white-yellow wings beating against green leaves and blue sky. We too have been released and, basking in the hot sun on top of the world, feel a lightness that if possible would express itself in flight.

There are more *papillons* this year, Roger tells us, because of all the rain. One restaurant was flooded three times. Roger and his wife Catherine, Monsieur Lassus's daughter, are overseeing the villa this year. Their wiry terrier, Kiskil, busies himself around the villa as if investigating a crime scene.

The shrieks of the wild peacocks in the valley are the very opposite of the gentle cooing of the doves along the cliff wall. A rooster crows, baby goats cry, jeeps and scooters honk on the road below. There is the smell of jasmine.

At lunch, small tawny hawks drift above the veranda. They hover still as death. One turns yards from us, flashing its checkered breast, its lunch, a tiny lizard, hanging from its beak. Could it be the lizard I saw earlier devouring a moth?

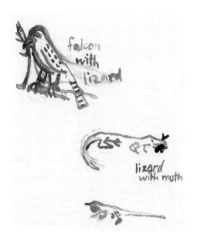

falcon with lizard

lizard with moth

Today is Carnaval. A parade of floats leads a masked crowd through the streets of Gustavia. Women and children in traditional Creole dress dance to beating drums and music blasting from speakers. The festival is an excuse for kissing, cross-dressing, drinking beer and rum, and dancing at Le Select. We run into Jean-Pierre dressed in a Mauritanian shirt and Bernadette in cat mask and *Cats* T-shirt.

"I'm so happy to see you," he says. "Come to Shell
Beach for the burning of *le roi.*"

At Maya's, the staff is dressed in jazzy sexy costumes.
They pose for pictures. Randy's idea of a costume is to
wear his shirttail out. He sits down at our table. "A lot of
people come for the glitz. They don't find it. No casino, no

golf course, not a lot of clubs. It's casual and low-key."

"What about that place where people dance on the tables?" Sarah asks.

"I haven't done that since college," I say.

"Isn't that when you broke your ankle?"

I almost run into a motor scooter on the way into town this morning. A large dog sits on the back of the scooter, like a co-pilot. Sarah finds Radio St. Barth on the radio. She sings along to a pop song.

"Not Lionel Ritchie?"

"Eloise is dating his bass man."

"Tiny Eloise?"

At the bakery, along with food for lunch, we get a bag of croissants. Sarah finishes one before we're halfway back up the mountain. I glance over at her.

"All about the freshness." She scrapes crumbs from her chin.

Jean-Pierre and Bernadette now live in a house in Colombier that overlooks the sea and an armada of boats. A big oil painting of three Caribbean women rests on an easel by an open window. The room smells of paint and turpentine. On the porch table are two papayas picked from a tree next to the railing. Cottony clouds float in the blue and gray sky.

Jean-Pierre opens a bottle of wine for Wendy and Bernadette. He pours Pastis ("one finger wide") into tall glasses. He fills them with water and hands me a glass. "Salut." Pistachios are passed. Silky cats rub against chairs. "He loves her," Jean-Pierre says, "but she doesn't love him. He brings her mice and lizards, but she scratches him."

Bernadette, a physical therapist, is thin and pretty with curls falling over her forehead. "Jean-Pierre and I stayed with a friend and her children and four cats during Luis. In one bedroom with water coming under the doors. *Le vent* gave us headaches and earaches. The pressure. Her husband was on a catamaran at sea."

"*Les baleines,* the whales, pass by every day this time of year. Would you like to see more of my paintings?"

Almost all are of women in patterned turbans and skirts. Settings are tropical streets and rooms or Turkish baths. "I sell everything I paint."

"An Ingres of the West Indies."

"*J'adore Ingres,*" he says.

At Le Repaire by the harbor we eat *carpaccio de poisson* as motorcycles roar down the street. An aristocratic English couple cheerily relive past love affairs over bright red *langouste*. David smokes a cigar while we walk along the boardwalk. A sleek black-bottomed sailboat from London is lashed to the pier. We pass the blind man who walks through town at night.

"*Bon soir, monsieur.*"

"*Bon soir.*" The man smiles in our direction. He taps his cane.

"Comment allez-vous?"
"Très bien, merci. Qu'elle heure est-il?"
"Il est dix heures."
"Merci. C'est une belle soirée."
"Oui, une belle soirée."

Robin MacNeil sits at a table across from two women of a certain age. He's not asking questions about important issues, he's having dinner. But after watching him for so many years on public television, you think for a moment he is. He's pretty good at candlelight conversation too, it seems. They're smiling and laughing. Certainly it's permissible to forget about the news for a while. That's why we're here.

man + woman
lying on beach
talking to each other

We climb the rocky hill to Saline. When we reach the grassy dune at the top we kick off our espadrilles and trip down the sandy hill to the sea. The beach is long and wide. It's not crowded. We spread towels and go for a walk. We pass others walking: couples confessing, solitary souls meditating.

A black Scottie watches a French boy and girl swat a ball back and forth. Its head goes back and forth as if at a tennis match. It stands over the ball when it lands in the sand. At one end of the beach are the all-browns, crisp as rotisserie chickens. We swim. The water is calm, there is a sandy bottom.

When we return to our towels we discover that Caroline Kennedy and her husband are camped out next to us. They lie on their towels alone, reading quietly. "Just like anybody else enjoying the beach," Wendy whispers.

"Someone's probably got a camera out."

Eddy is the epitome of laid-back islander. His eponymous restaurant is one of the most popular on the island. He has a goatee and ponytail and a thin handsome face. Five feet tall at most, he stands at the table, in shorts and white linen shirt.

"What do you recommend?"

"The goat." He speaks softly.

Tables in the garden under the palms are full as are the tables under the thatched roof in front of the open kitchen. Eddy sits at a large round

table, a tiny guru, surrounded by friends and customers. One sun-darkened man with a ponytail has a guitar. Maybe he has to sing for his supper.

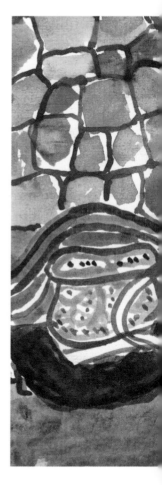

Years ago, Eddy's father Marius, a one-time mayor of Gustavia, opened Le Select under the huge flamboyant tree in the center of town. Arguably it's the heart of local St. Barts. The funky bar is almost always open, motorcycles line the street, and on many weekends a band plays.

Eddy circles back at the end of our meal. "Would you like a rum?

"What do you do in summer?"

"We travel. Two months with our children. Travel is important. But we always come back. St. Barts is paradise."

A band is playing at the new Jungle Café on the harbor. The place is dark and stylish but not very full. "Chinese wallpaper in the loo," Wendy says. She looks stylish in her white Italian shirt and black pants.

David orders a gin and tonic. Two Cuban cigars stick

out of his shirt pocket.

"Pretty grown up," I say to him. He's 21.

Sarah's hair is a fountain of yellow curls. "What color are your nails?"

"Cerise. Dad, I'm a girl, I can have long nails. David, do you want to dance?"

"There's nobody dancing."

"It's early." They go out on the empty dance floor.

The gendarmes are strict about motorcycle helmets. Jean-Pierre's equestrian bowler is chic but useless. The young wear thick practical helmets. They zip by on their scooters, girl behind the boy, brown, cool, immortal. They head to the beach, beer in a basket, scruffy dog between the boy's bare feet. Old Triumphs and BMWs are around too, usually outside a repair shop. At night, boys race down the straightaways, Rue de la Republique or Rue Jeanne d'Arc, front wheels high off the ground. They're trying to take off, to fly free of their tiny island.

Yves is another Frenchman who fled the homeland. Lucas, his son, sits on his lap and takes a small sip from a glass of Champagne. He prefers *le langue du chat,* the tongue of the cat, a cookie coated in chocolate.

We're all sipping Champagne. Yves's small boat,

which he piloted from Brazil where he met Ana, sits in the harbor. The cramped interior is not for the claustrophobic. Sailboats are a combination of freedom and prison. Through the cabin door I see the lights of town.

There is only one good doctor on the island. If you have a heart attack, you are taken to St. Martin in a helicopter. Ana went first to St. Martin then to Guadeloupe to have her baby. Lucas was born during a hurricane.

I tell Lucas that I am *un grand mouton.* He looks at me quizzically. When I let out a long baaaah, he laughs loudly.

I open my sketchbook. I look at the varieties of flesh on the beach. Some is poetry, most is prose. All of it is human, drawn to this hilly mecca in the Caribbean by the gods of sun and sea. A French woman rubs lotion on her breasts. Near her an English woman with leathery skin reads a book.

Two girls run up wet from the sea and stick their faces in the sand. They laugh at each other's grainy masks then run back into the water. I glance in the direction of a heavy sprawled sunbather with his manhood splayed on his thigh like an old root vegetable.

There's a frog in the cistern. Its croaking is loud and eerie. Unable to sleep, I sit in the living room reading at 3:00 a.m. The rain stops, moonlight fills the valley. In the morning we lift a wooden cover from the floor in the pantry. Sitting on a pole in the cistern is the frog. *"La petit grenouille,"* Ana says, *"fait un grand bruit."*

Yves arrives with a net on a long pole. He can't catch it. It's a hot day. We read by the pool. Piaf, Monsieur Lassus's Siamese cat, naps on the tiles. The lizards but not the frog come out to play.

A thin man prances around in underpants, preening for his friends as he sorts through a rack of linen pants. Claude, the florid, garrulous owner of Images, a men's store in Gustavia, rolls his eyes.

"Vous êtes magnifique!" He spreads his arms as if to embrace Sarah and Wendy. *"Et, monsieur, vous êtes magnifique. Bienvenue, bienvenue."*

"Merci." I pick up a shirt.

"J'aime les chemises."

"Moi aussi."

Claude rubs his forehead. *"Je suis un peu fatiguée.* I want to sell store. *C'est comme...a heavy roach, un roche. Je veux vivre comme un paysan.* Like a pheasant. A simple life."

At a loss for words or rather taken by Claude's melancholy confession and amusing Franglais, I look at the ties. "If you can't find tie you like, I suicide."

I picture a man hanging from a bright tie instead of a frayed rope. I buy two shirts. He gives me a tie. *"S'il vous plaît, un cadeau.* You don't wear on the island. Wear at a party. *Une fête avec les belles dames. Chez vous."*

"Regardez. Un arc-en-ciel." Ana points at the rainbow above the mountains across the valley.

"A full rainbow. *C'est beau.*"

Ana points down the hill below us at a patch of open ground. *"Regardez. Près de la petite ferme. Un pon."*

"Peacock!"

Wendy gets the binoculars.

"Spreading its tail."

"Il cherche une femme."

"Rainbow and peacock at the same time. *En même temps.*"

"C'est le paradis." Ana smiles her beautiful smile.

Sarah's boyfriend Michael arrives from Houston. We go to Maya's for dinner. "My grandmother was married eight times."

"Is that legal?"

"It's legal in Texas."

"Anything's legal in Texas," Sarah says.

Handsome with black hair and easy-going charm, Michael could be John Travolta's younger brother. "My Dad grew up in a trailer park in Odessa. Now he's a producer for CBS in Tampa and drives a Porsche."

Sarah orders a glass of Champagne.

"And for you?"

"Crown and Coke, please, ma'am," Michael says.

Bernadette tells Sarah and Michael about nightlife on the island. "First you have dinner then you go to Le Petit Club. It's very small, there's lots of cigarette smoke and loud music. Then you go to the nightclub Le Feeling. It opens after midnight. You have to wear black and white."

"That's just down the hill from the villa."

"Très simple, très primitif," Jean-Pierre says.

"I don't have anything white," Michael says.

"Pas de problème. They always let beautiful people in."

frigate birds

Charivari is a 44-foot sailboat that we've chartered for the day. Yo-Yo and Natalie are the crew. Yo-Yo is Swiss and has sailed the seas and cycled the continents.

Settled now, he has lived on the island for ten years with his wife and two sons. He has blond curly hair and a quiet air of competence and confidence.

"I come from a family of florists. Five generations."

"I'm a florist," Wendy says, delighted.

"We sail first in the direction of Île Fourchue."

Natalie lets out the sails. Yo-Yo turns off the engine. There is only the sound of the wind. "The best moment in sailing."

We pass by the former Rockefeller house on Colombier, at the northwest end of the island. Reachable only by boat or foot (or by helicopter), it's now owned by the head of Coca-Cola. We leave the Caribbean and enter the Atlantic. The water turns a dark ultramarine blue. Frigatebirds drift high in the sky.

"The frigatebird almost never beats its wings. It just

rides the drafts, up and down like a roller coaster. It dives faster than any bird."

Natalie is from Lyon. She came to the island like so many young for adventure and romance. They work in shops and restaurants and live in small hot rooms all for the chance to go to full moon parties and eat fresh fish and swim in the sea. Most go back after a while. Many stay and drink their wine and smoke their cigarettes and are never cold again.

"Wind is 25 knots, waves 4 to 6 feet. Depth 25 meters."

We drop anchor in a cove at rocky Île Fourchue. "A hermit used to live here," Natalie says. "Now only goats. They eat everything. Would be a good place for a disco. It's for sale."

It's a good place for snorkeling. Sarah and Michael flipper off in one direction, Wendy and I in another. We are quickly lost in the silence and dreamy beauty. We tap each other and point at iridescent fish and spreads of coral.

After lunch in the bay at Colombier, we sail back to Gustavia. Under sail, thin and sleek on the water, is the

famous *Endeavour*. "The most beautiful boat in the world. Built in the 20s. Its mast is 50 meters high. It was recently restored."

We pass the wreck of a boat destroyed by a hurricane. The storm also sank the only crane on the island big enough to salvage it. The boat lies ruined on a giant rock at the entrance to the harbor.

In a shop in St. Jean, Sarah kneels to pat a shaggy dog sprawled under an air conditioner. "He had a walk on the beach," the shopkeeper says, "saw his girlfriend. Now he sleeps. Later, he goes to the restaurant. They give him food. It's a good life."

"Life on St. Barts is good for people and dogs."

We buy a CD by Kaoma, a French/Brazilian pop group. Back at the villa, we swim, then open a bottle of wine. I put on the CD. The first song is "Chacha La Vie." Sarah and Wendy immediately start dancing to the catchy music. "What about lunch?"

"Can't stop now." Sarah leads Michael and Wendy in a conga line to the terrace.

"Chacha la vie," David says.

"Je vous monte le chemin," Jean-Pierre says. He is sitting

on his *moto* in front of the airport. He pulls on his polo helmet and is quickly on the road. We follow him up the hills to Caramouche, a secluded haven of villas. We stop at the house of Bernard Chatain, an architect/painter born in Algeria and a friend of Jean-Pierre's.

The house is on a steep hill overlooking St. Jean and Lorient. Designed by Bernard, it is part traditional St. Barts, part modern. The open-air living and dining rooms are painted blue and red and furnished with bleached wood chairs and tables and faded fabrics.

"You have a beautiful house."

"I'm going to sell it. I'm moving to New York. My son was just accepted at Parsons." He has thick dark hair and a heady intensity. "The middle-class in the U.S. is more accepting of art than the middle-class in France is."

Hurricanes figure in every island conversation, especially the bad hurricanes. "The roof of the house was blown off by Luis. I tried to hold the bedroom door shut for hours. Then I went to the basement. The sound was incredible. Like standing under a Boeing."

Bernard's neighbors, Bernie Rogers and Mary Warner, walk over, carrying drinks. Mary's young son is trying to catch lizards with a net. A tall handsome man, Bernie is friendly and WASPish somewhat in the manner of George Plimpton. "I'm in my post-corporate period." He grew up in Chicago and knows some of the same people Wendy and her family know.

Bernadette comes from work. *"Ça va?"* She busses our cheeks. "You must practice your French. My mother taught English. I rebelled, I learned Spanish."

Outside under a gazebo, we drink and watch the sunset. "I have been coming to St. Barts for 20 years," Bernie says. "I still love it."

Mary works for a photography agency in Aspen. "I am a photographer myself, and a painter." She's down to earth and has a sense of humor, qualities all the more attractive when you know that her mother was the granddaughter of Andrew Mellon and her father, John Warner, was a longtime U.S. senator and a husband of Elizabeth Taylor.

off gouverneur

"You're going native."

"Sarong of Myself. A poem about going native."

We have drinks by the pool before lunch. I ceremo-

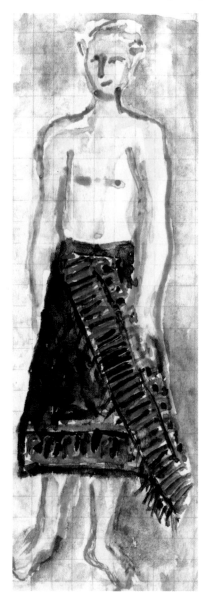

niously carry out a tray with two glasses of Martini Rouge and a bowl of Triangolini crackers. I offer a glass to Wendy. *"Madame, s'il tu plaît."*

"Not exactly a white bistro apron. But you look very nice in your sarong."

"Chacha la vie."

"Avez-vous des timbres plus...?"

"Plus jolis?"

"Oui, plus jolis."

"Non." A Gallic shrug. The clerk hands me the five plain stamps.

From the cash machine outside the post office, I take an orange 100-franc note with Paul Cézanne on it. I also get blue 50-franc notes with Antoine de Saint-Exupéry on them and purple brown 20-franc notes with Claude Debussy. What will the new Euro notes look

like? More bland than pretty, I'm sure, and certainly not honoring an artist or composer.

"We saw an iguana near the church. It was eating flowers," Sarah says. "Very dinosaurish."

"*L'iguane aime l'hibiscus,*" Ana says.

"Cruise ships are in," David says. "Streets are crowded. At one store, a guy stuck his head in the door and asked, 'Where's the nude beach?'"

Lucas shows his toy helicopter to David. "*Comment dit-on* helicopter *en français?*" Lucas makes flying noises.

"*Hélicoptère,*" Ana says.

"*En portugais?*"

"*Helicóptero.*"

"I like *helicóptero* better."

"*Cóptero,*" Lucas says. He runs around holding the little plane high. "*Cóptero. Cóptero.*"

Sudden gusts whip up the sand, stinging the skin. The waves are high. I am tossed about like a giant doll, helpless but exhilarated. The sun starts to set behind the hill at the end of the bay. David and Sarah walk along the beach from

light to shadow. Laughing and talking, they are drenched by
the high-splashing tide.

Back at the house, we wash away sand and salt. Wendy,
wrapped in a towel, brushes her long wet hair. David and
I drink Heineken from little bottles, just enough for a
parched throat. I have a small glass of *rhum vieux* from
Martinique. It's dark and smooth and perfectly of the place,
of *"le terroir Caraibe."*

Day eases into night quiet as a cat. The air is soft and
cool, the light ethereal. Clouds gray in the violet sky. I
stand alone on the terrace, looking out at
the darkening mountains, faint stars, lamp
light in the valley. What's the word? It's
more than peaceful. Something not often
felt that always catches you by surprise. It's
contentment. When outside aligns with
inside.

One morning I meet Taki, a Japanese
friend of Jean-Pierre's. Taki is a dentist who
wants to be a painter. He is an expert on
reconstructing teeth and travels the world from his home
in Florida giving lectures. For the last two years he has been
living on St. Barts making paintings. Jean-Pierre has hired
a model and we have gathered with pencils and paper in
the living room of his house. An old four-masted schooner
moored in the harbor is visible through the window.

The model's name is France. She has a ring on her
toe and *un bronzage partout* (an all-over tan). She's quite glib.
Everybody lights a cigarette, including France. Jean-Pierre
and Taki draw slowly, realistically. I work in a sketchier,
faster way. "His pencil does not leave the paper." France
nods towards me. *"C'est fou.* It's mad."

"I want to be more spontaneous," Jean-Pierre says. "I spend an hour working on a shoulder." I go with him to his new studio, a five-minute drive from his house. He built the studio, a single small room with a porch, in the garden of a friend. Outside is a pool of guppies and orchids. He's working on a big painting of three Caribbean women. "My clientele always want the same thing."

We sit on a broad wooden bench and talk. He shows me a book of Egon Schiele's work. "I order canvas and paint from New York and Paris." He drops another cigarette

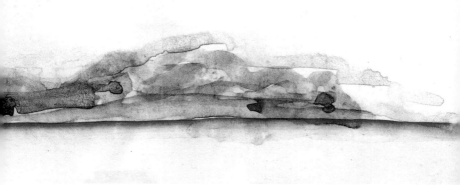

into the Moroccan ashtray. "Taki is a nice man but he is unhappy. He's getting divorced and he is tired of his work."

Jean-Pierre suddenly swings a pink racket through the air. There is a pop and the smell of something burning. The racket is electrified. *"Il y a beaucoup de moustiques."*

Bernie folds up his reading glasses and puts them in a tiny tortoise-shell case. "I have six children scattered across the U.S." It's raining, which makes the busy harbor restaurant all the more intimate and lively. "I wrote a short story when I was at Yale and it was accepted by *The Atlantic Monthly*. First time I submitted something."

"Why didn't you keep writing?"

"I'm easily distracted." He does have stories to tell. White-haired and debonair, he's had a full life. "I keep a car on the island. It's made in India, costs less than $5000, and lasts four or five years."

The rain lets up. We walk along the boardwalk. "I was almost part of the crew on the *Endeavour* for one of its transatlantic crossings. It didn't work out." Two beefy yachts from the Bahamas are tied up at the pier. Each has a helicopter perched on it. "His and hers," Bernie says.

"It mattered how a man ate, how he lived, how he organized his day. It mattered for the sake not of his image but his soul." I read this in *Nietzsche in Turin* by Lesley Chamberlain.

My day unfolds in more or less the same way every day. Swim in the pool before breakfast, remark upon the ripeness of the melon, scatter crumbs for the doves, mind the cactus on the trail, drink wine at lunch, read a few pages of a well-written book, let the watercolors go where they will, swim in the sea, order the orange pound cake, embrace the ones I love, walk the harbor (saying hello to the blind man if he passes), bless the breeze and the stars.

Drinks at Taki's. His house is within walking distance of Jean-Pierre's. Quiet but charming, Taki shows us his paintings in his tiny hot studio. Braque-like still lifes, Maillol-like nudes.

"Taki and I decided we drink too much whiskey. We're cutting back to two times a week. We sometimes make sushi together."

"Yellow-tailed snapper are raised in captivity in Japan," Taki says. "When they are young they are called to their food with a whistle. Trained like Pavlov's dog. Then they are released into the wild sea. Later, when they are larger and ready to eat, they are whistled back. Three-quarters of them return."

Eveline gives us a box of chocolate. *"Un cadeau pour vous. À la prochaine."*

"Merci, Eveline. À la prochaine."

We have a glass of farewell wine with Ana and Yves in *"la petite maison"* above the villa. Ana shows us a photograph. *"La maison de Monsieur Lassus dans le Pays Basque."*

melon
from
Guadeloupe

Lucas sticks olives on the ends of his fingers. *"Donne moi cinq."* He eats the entire plate of olives and promptly throws up on his overalls.

"Our last night. Of course we came here for dinner."

"It's always nice to have you," Maya says.

"How about some shrub?" Randy says, putting two glasses down. "Will we see you next year?"

"As long as you're pouring shrub."

We walk along the harbor looking at boats, enjoying the breeze. "Still have to pack."

"Remember I'm not carrying your rocks in my bag."

The small plane races down the runway. From our seats, we can see the pilots in the cockpit. The plane lifts off well before the beach and turns sharply left. We look down at the island, green and whole in the blue sea. Straining to look back, I see our mountain.

FOUR

Frangipani

The island is in drought.

The gardens are brown, the cistern is low. The view
from the mountain house is bewitching as ever. Roger and
Catharine show us the satellite TV they have installed along
with a fax machine and new four-poster beds. They've
provided Champagne, fruit, flowers, and fancy soaps. Kiskil
pads around, barking happily.

"Quite a journey." We lift glasses at Maya's.

Yesterday, when we got into a taxi at Newark Airport,
I told the driver our hotel was in SoHo. "Where's SoHo?"
she said.

"No more taxis. From now on car service."

Leaving the hotel for the airport this morning before
dawn, the Russian taxi driver took a wrong turn and was
well on his way to Clinton before we turned around.

"We're here now. On the island away from urban woes."

"Not to mention the worst winter in history."

"A few days in the sun will burn it from memory."

"Poetic."

The island is one big smoothie. I take a sip from a glass of mango and banana whipped to a froth. Morning sun brightens the valley. We drive down the mountain and take a walk along the road to Saline, Route de Saline.

A man jogs by. "Is that David Letterman? I think he has a house near here."

As I turn to look, a large parrot swoops down over our heads. It lands in a tree and cocks its brilliant blue head to get a better view.

"Look how yellow its chest is," Wendy says.

"And how sharp its bill."

"Must be the one from Le Tamarin. Isn't it called a macaw?"

"I thought they were friendly."

It swoops again coming even closer to our heads. Then again. "It's dive-bombing us." I wave my hat as it turns for another go. We run down the road. "It thinks it's a game. Those claws could take a big hunk out of a scalp."

"Does it dive-bomb David Letterman?"

"'It's difficult to believe in death before sunset.'" I quote from Graham Greene's *Journey Without Maps,* which I'm reading. "Except when Captain Hook attacks you on your morning walk."

"I doubt that a macaw has ever killed anyone."

A dove coos, the soothing notes sounding as if blown gently through a shell. With a flutter of wings, it lands near my poolside chair. I toss bread crumbs. I like having it around. Clouds from a child's book, puffy and white, drift in rows above the horizon. At the horizon, pale sky meets dark sea in a mist of heat and haze. Islands break the tyranny of the straight line. The sun, exactly overhead, pricks your skin, your eyelids. Time for a swim.

Last night we watched from the veranda the full moon rise in the eastern sky. It was a voluptuous yellow-orange. A giant invisibly tethered balloon, it rose slowly but steadily above the mountains. There was something shocking and primeval about it. Maybe because we had never watched it closely, rising moment by moment in its ancient path. Later, high in the sky, it turned a chaste white. It seemed aloof, but its ghostly light spread like a benevolent hand across land and water and our upturned faces.

More from *Journey Without Maps:*
The village women danced to us that evening in starlight to the music of rattles. It was not a lovely dance. . .but they were cheerful and happy and we were happy, too, as they slapped

and rattled and laughed and pranced, and we drank warm
boiled water with whisky and the juice of limes, and the
timelessness, the irresponsibility, the freedom of Africa began
to touch us at last.

We have lunch at the villa with friends from home.
We sit on our terrace overlooking the sea. "Life is all about
the view, isn't it?" Sally says.

"If everyone had a view of water there would be no wars."

"Let's start with everyone having clean water to drink,"
Michael, the doctor, says.

"This is a pretty incredible view," David, Michael's
partner, says. "I certainly don't feel like going into battle.
Could I have a touch more rosé, please?"

"What is that screeching?" Dan asks.

"Wild peacocks."

"I didn't know peacocks screeched."

Sally and Dan, architects and long-time friends, are single. David and Michael tease them about hanging out at Le Deck and Le Petit Club.

"You'd think it would be easier on a Caribbean island."

"You mean, sex on the beach and all that," Michael says.

"Isn't that a drink?"

"It's hard to be single," Sally says. "And a woman."

"It's hard to be married," Dan says. "How do you guys do it?"

"It's all about the view."

"What does that mean?"

"No war. We share the same view. Point of view."

"Just a few battles," Wendy says.

David and Sarah arrive from New York on Sunday in time for a late lunch. They had the small plane from St. Martin to themselves for the ten-minute flight.

"The Vermeer show at the Met is fantastic. And I saw these huge photographs at MOMA by Andreas Gursky. Ten or fifteen feet wide. Work places, buildings, landscapes taken from a distance. Amazing."

"He's got two girlfriends, both from Baltimore."

"Two women from Baltimore. Could be a play or short story."

"Or trouble."

"No, nothing serious."

Sarah talks about Eric, a friend whose family has a whole-sale fish business. "Have you ever held a 225-pound halibut?"

"Have you?"

"No, but Eric has."

"Was it for the famous Jersey Halibut Heft?"

We spread towels on the *plage* at Gouverneur late in the afternoon. David and Sarah walk to the end of the bay. Four boys race into the water together and somersault into the waves. "I can do that."

"You haven't done a somersault since you were three."

I run down to the water and bend over, resting my head on the sand. "I need a hand. Give me a little push." Wendy pushes me from behind. I land on my back just as a wave sweeps in. I spit out sand. "Thanks."

"More like a somerflop."

The water shortage is serious. The new desalination plant will not be completed until the end of the year. Marc, the pool man, talks with Roger about how long water in the cistern will last. We take our books out to the pool as Marc scoops out leaves and dead insects. "Going to rain like crazy in October," he says to us. "That's the fucking problem."

"All the books you choose are sad," Wendy says.

"All good books are sad."

"Jane Austen is not sad," Sarah says.

David reads to Sarah by the pool from *A Passage to India.*

"You should put cream in your fur. Your chest is getting red." She climbs out of the pool, wringing her long hair.

"Your curls are gone."

She lies on the tiles, her face turned to the sun, and talks with her eyes closed. "I met a beautiful woman with a beautiful name, Aithana. She lives here for six months then she goes to Bali for six months. I met her at the black moon party last night. I also met a chef who works for a couple who spends four months a year in Aspen, four months in New York, two months in Paris, and two months in St. Barts."

"That's 14 months."

"No, it isn't. It's amazing how people go from one groovy place to another."

"Jet set jets on."

Sarah is a bit of jet-setter. She goes out every night. We rented a second car for her social rambles. One night she's with Sophie, another with Mario, another with a group at a club. "This is perfectly perfect," Wendy says.

"What is perfectly perfect?"

"This moment lying in the sun with all of you. It's perfectly perfect."

Before lunch, Wendy and I go to see Randy and Maya's house in the valley. "How was the house?" Sarah asks when we return.

Head in the Clouds
(The Thinker)

"I loved it," Wendy says. "They built it. It's Creole-style, yellow and pale blue wood. Not pretentious, nothing like all the fancy modern houses."

"Which are pretty ugly."

"You can see it from here. The group of bungalows in a garden of bougainvillea and hibiscus. There's a wall of books in the living room. The only thing missing is a view."

"Maya says it's simple, which it is. That's why it's so appealing.

"Their puppy was high."

"It ate marijuana."

A day of sailing with Yo-Yo. Good winds and good weather; sea turtles and flying fish are our escorts. David and Wendy spot a barracuda when we stop to snorkel at Île Fourchue. We have lunch in the bay at Colombier beneath the old Rockefeller estate. "Soon after it was sold for many millions of dollars, it was hit by a hurricane," Yo-Yo says. Houses and hurricanes: high prices, high winds.

Hurricanes used to hit the island once every 30 years, Yo-Yo tells us. "There have been five in the last six years. I took my boat to Antigua during Hurricane Lenny. The wind destroyed my mainsail, but at least I got to a protected cove. Some boats didn't make it. Some people didn't make it."

Yo-Yo lived in Polynesia for three years before settling in St. Barts. His oldest boy is in boarding school in

Guadeloupe. "His first room," Yo-Yo says. "He's always lived on a boat." When he asked his sons if they wanted to move to Switzerland, they said, "No way." He joins a group of divers every year to pick up litter in the sea around the island. "In the old days, people dumped cars and refrigerators in the water."

We motor slowly into Gustavia. "I love this harbor. It's gentle, welcoming. I never tire of it."

"You grew up in Switzerland, land of mountains, and ended up being a sailor."

"True." He pauses, thinking. He looks at me and says simply, "I'm glad I did."

L'etang de St. Jean is a shallow pond of brackish water that somehow manages to support an ecosystem of fish, frogs, and birds. A "hedge"of thick vegetation separates it from a road, which though busy is flat and a good place to walk. Heavy brown pelicans dive full bore. Egrets and sandpipers wait calmly before striking.

Around the bend from the pond is the "athletic zone"—the public pool, soccer field and track, judo and archery clubs, tennis and volleyball courts. Sailing and water sports are one thing, but you also need land sports to keep island families and athletic types active. It's always busy. Walking or driving by on the way to the grocery store or to the airport, you see boys in judo suits, men and women aiming arrows at targets. You hear an instructor's whistle at the pool, the thump of foot on a soccer ball.

David has brought the DVD *A Touch of Evil*. "A little film noir in paradise. Just what we need."

One of the many brilliant scenes takes place when Orson Welles, who both directs and acts (he plays Quinlan, a police captain in a Mexican-American border town), shows up late at night at the brothel run by Tanya, a prostitute played by Marlene Dietrich. Porcine and grizzled, he stands in the doorway eating a candy bar. She dries dishes and puffs on a cigarette that never leaves her mouth. She looks ravishing, despite her dark wig.

> *"I didn't recognize you," she says. "You should lay off those candy bars."*
>
> *"Either the candy or the hooch. Must say I wish it was your chili I was gettin' fat on. Anyway, you're sure lookin' good."*
>
> *"You're a mess, honey. . ."*
>
> *". . . Well, when this case is over I'll come around and sample some of your chili."*
>
> *"Better be careful, it may be too hot for you."*

Awake at dawn to the sound of crickets. Pale gray clouds in a pale yellow sky. A sugarbird flies into our bedroom. It flies around frantically until it crashes into a window. I carry the tiny stunned creature to the veranda. It rests for a moment then flies down the hillside. "They're actually called bananaquits. That's their official ornithological name."

"I like sugarbirds better. Will it be all right?"

"I think so."

We are serenaded at breakfast by a rooster and a peacock. We gather with our bibles (novels and biographies) and take places around the pool. A rapid fluttering of wings, the dove is beside my chair. I look out at the clouds coalescing in the peerless sky. For some reason, I think of the line from *White Mischief*— the movie (I have not read the book): "Oh, God. Not another fucking beautiful day," uttered by Alice de Janzé, the flamboyant American heiress who was part of the decadent Happy Valley crowd in Kenya between the wars. Living only for pleasure, even in a beautiful place, is not good for your health. Alice shot herself and her lover.

David does his short laps. He wears goggles. "Everyone says David has nice hair," Sarah says.

"Don't I have nice hair?"

"You have a nice head, Dad."

"Here's a good line." I read from my book. "'Books still keep me afloat, but a good lunch is a great levitator, and far more enduring.'"

"What book is that?"

"*Lunch with Elizabeth David.* Unfortunately it goes downhill after the second page."

"Speaking of lunch."

"Time to levitate," David says.

les
sucriers

"He was *un peinteur voyageur,* a traveling painter. His name
was Georges François. I am Christian. Welcome to the gallery."
Christian tells us he bought hundreds of the artist's paintings
and drawings from his widow. "All of the remaining works.
We hope to have an exhibition in New York." Christian, portly,
bearded, speaks in a steady monologue of baritone French. His
wife Christine shows us portfolios of the artist's work. We sift
through the many drawings, watercolors, and gouaches. We set
aside several pieces.

"Very much like Delacroix's African watercolors," I say.

"François lived in Africa as well as in the West Indies. He
painted in the first half of the century. He was very prolific, as
you can see. He lived a long time. What do you think of the oil
paintings?"

"I like the drawings better."

"These pieces would look wonderful in a house on the
island," Wendy says.

"You don't have a villa here?" Christine says.

"No, we just rent one."

"Can you come back tomorrow?" Christian asks. "I will have your pieces wrapped up." He lights a cigar. "I'm glad you like the work. He's a wonderful artist."

"To Georges François, the traveling painter."

Lunch with Randy and Maya at Do Brazil, the restaurant next to Plage des Galets (Shell Beach). The handsome Algerian waiter says to Wendy, *"Vous êtes la maman de Sarah?"*

"Yes, I have a daughter named Sarah."

"I love Sarah." He puts his hand to his heart. "She looks like you."

Maya and Randy drop ice cubes into their glasses of rosé. The fish is cooked in a salty crust. Daytrippers lounge on the beach, which is covered in tiny shells and within walking distance of the harbor. "We went to Las Vegas last year on our holiday," Maya says, "to see Cirque de Soleil. Then we went to see the canyons."

A tall suave Frenchman stops to say hello to Randy and Maya. "BouBou opened this restaurant with Yannick Noah," Randy says. "Do you know Wendy and David?"

"I know your daughter."

"Everybody knows Sarah," Maya says.

Ana, Yves, and Lucas have moved back to the island from Brazil. We gather on the porch of Jean-Pierre's and Bernadette's house overlooking Colombier. On the table are plates of ham and salmon, bowls of nuts and carrots. Jean-Pierre opens a bottle of Champagne.

Lucas, now six, is still a beautiful boy. "Is that Spiderman?" Sarah asks him.

"Oui," he says proudly. *"Il est l'homme d'araignée."*

Lucas

Ana, her hair in corn rows, looks lovely in a long white dress. Yves is thinner, grayer. "We try to build a life on the island," he says. *"Mais c'est difficile."*

"I am having an exhibition in Japan," Jean-Pierre says. Dapper in white pants and high-top brogues (no socks), he shows us his "Japanese drawings." The sensitively drawn nudes on blue paper are studies for the paintings that will be in the show.

"I love your outfit," Wendy says to Bernadette. She's wearing an opalescent "Oriental" jacket and blue pants.

"Merci beaucoup," she says. "We are in an Eastern mood now. I am studying Thai massage."

"Bon anniversaire, Jean-Pierre," Ana says and lifts her glass.

"He just turned 60," Bernadette says. "We celebrated in France."

"I want you to meet Quitterie," Jean-Pierre says to David. "She is a young Parisian artist. She will be in Brooklyn this summer. She looks like the actress Juliet Binoche."

"Be happy to."

An old island woman in a long skirt and straw hat stoops over the rocks on Grand Fond. She picks up debris that has washed ashore—sailor's rope, plastic bucket, bottles. Some of it she puts in a bag. She has long braids down her back and is surprisingly nimble.

A hot afternoon. I swim in my usual dogged way at Gouverneur. Wendy, an excellent swimmer, prefers to paddle about. "I don't want to get my hair wet. It takes too much villa water to wash it."

Our table overlooks the dark water of the bay. Spotlights shine through the lapping waves. A large school of tarpon swims into view. We sip end-of-dinner rum. Eden Rock is the island's oldest and most storied hotel. Originally the home of Rémy de Haenen (who, in addition to landing the first plane on the island, was a smuggler and mayor), it sits alluringly atop a stony headland on St. Jean Bay. David Rockefeller, an early devotée of St. Barts, slept here as de Haenen's guest. So did Greta Garbo and Howard Hughes. In 1946, the mythic de Haenen founded the Compagnie Aérienne Antillaise, the first airline in the area.

"Island style," I say. "Never far from a drink or a smile."

"The great painter of women, a lover of women." A big blonde man sets small glasses of rum on the table, smiles at

Jean-Pierre. Jean-Pierre smiles through a haze of cigarette smoke and looks at Bernadette.

"The woman who works here used to serve Jean-Pierre his morning coffee and pastry. That was before I met him."

"That was a long time ago."

"Not that long."

The blonde man is owner with his brother of *Les Grains de Sel*, the small restaurant near Saline popular with islanders.

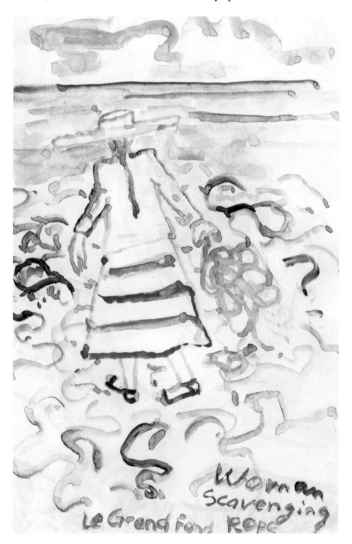

Woman Scavenging Le Grand Fond Rope

We sit on the porch enjoying a last get-together.

"Someone asked me for money," Bernadette says. "*Un étranger*. First time it's happened to me on the island."

"I remember being robbed by the customs man at the Brazil-Venezuela border," Jean-Pierre says. "When I arrived in Caracas I had to ask a stranger for help, for money."

"The island is changing."

"Yes, it is."

"Too many people."

"It's busier. But people on the island are better off. More prosperity, more to go around."

"Things are more expensive."

"There are more robberies."

"At least the man did not try to rob me."

Sarah persuades us to let her stay another week. David is already back in New York. "I can stay with Randy and Maya."

"We'll look after her," Maya says. "She'll be fine."

"How will you get around?"

"Friends. I'm getting picked up in a few minutes."

"You haven't finished your pasta."

She throws back her head of yellow ringlets and stands up. "I'll see you in the morning."

"You're coming back to the house tonight, aren't you?"

"Yes, but you'll be asleep. What time do you leave tomorrow?"

Off she goes. We say goodbye to Randy and Maya and take a last walk along the harbor. A band plays at Le Select. A man in a tie-dye T-shirt sits on a bench by the water with a Yorkshire terrier perched on his stomach.

I gaze out the plane window at the stars in the night sky. Below are town lights, dark winding American rivers. I find in my notebook this line from *Swann's Way:*

> *The places that we have known belong now only to the little world of space on which we map them for our own convenience. None of them was ever more than a thin slice, held between the contiguous impressions that composed our life at that time; remembrance of a particular form is but regret for a particular moment; and houses, roads, avenues are as fugitive, alas, as the years.*

FIVE

The pharmacy is a good place to improve your French.

Pansement is French for dressing, *une coupure* is a cut, so
we learn today at the pharmacy in St. Jean. The pharmacist
suggests *medicament antiseptique* for *la blessure* (the wound) on
my foot incurred while walking barefooted on the rocky
path to Saline. French pharmacists are knowledgeable
and helpful. Pharmacies are stocked with everything you
need (and lots you don't) for health and grooming. Often
products are as aesthetically pleasing as they are useful.

Wendy buys a tortoise-shell comb. I buy a bottle of red
Botot mouthwash (*eau de bouche*). It was created, I read on the
elegant label, for Louis XV in 1755 by Dr. Julien Botot.
What we don't need is a bar of soap smelling of frangipani
or a lotion with flakes of gold leaf to make one's skin baby-
soft, but they find their way into the basket.

I smile when I hear Perry Como's warm voice oozing
through the speaker. He was one of my mother's favorite

singers. "Interesting choice of music." Andy Williams, another of my mother's favorites, sings "Quiet Nights and Quiet Stars."

The décor at Le Toiny is Indonesian-inspired: indigo fabrics, coffee brown furniture. As if on cue, a breeze ripples the water of the pool, which overlooks the sea. The atmosphere, like Perry's crooning, is suave and smooth. Everything in the restaurant and hotel has been fussed over.

A model-handsome waiter sprinkles powdered sugar over our blue dessert plates, creating white silhouettes of knife and fork. The small round *tiedeur* of chocolate has a sauce of carrots and basil.

"Even the cats are clean."

"They got two out of three. *Luxe et calme.*"

"*Pas volupté,*" Wendy says.

"What about hurricanes?"

"They're building houses stronger now."

"Wouldn't you want a Creole house painted a nice shade
of blue with porches wrapped around all four sides?"

"If you had a house in Lurin, you'd have the wind all the time not to mention the worst of a hurricane."

"But the view. You would have the view."

"We would need a nice garden."

"Lurin is quieter, not as busy."

"Maintenance is an issue."

"The housekeeper, the gardener, the pool man."

"We can't afford to buy something here."

"You could rent it out."

"A very wealthy man once told me that he always rents vacation houses. 'Better to rent someone's else folly,' he said, 'than to have to deal with your own.'"

"You wouldn't spend enough time here to justify buying."

"There's always Florida."

Sunbathe *au naturel* beneath heaven and hawks. A dip in the pool, really a large bathtub. It's Sunday. Roasted chicken on the terrace, valley gaping before us. The overripe mango is sweet and piney.

Massing clouds and heavy waves chase us from the beach at Gouverneur. Wendy's hazel eyes, auburn hair, red-brown skin are a palette of Scottish fall not Caribbean spring. "What color is your sarong? Persimmon?"

"Burnt sienna with a hint of orange."

"What's the other word?"

"*Pareo.* Worn by women and men."

"A kilt for the tropics."

We climb the hill to the lighthouse in Gustavia and look down at the harbor, which is like a three-sided box with one end open to the sea. Two kayakers, water bugs from this height, jockey for space with a white yacht, big as a building, easing its square fanny into a berth at the pier. In the opposite direction, a small plane, just meters above the road, approaches the airport, looking for all the world as if it will crash into the hillside.

"Next time I go to France I want to sail not fly," Jean-Pierre says. "I want to be in the middle of the ocean with nothing but water all around."

"You're not afraid?"

"No, I feel free. Incredibly free."

"What about living on an island? Do you feel isolated sometimes?"

"My favorite thing in the world is to sit at a bar looking out at the sea or at a harbor filled with boats."

Bernadette puts cheese on the table. "From Pays-Basque. My home region." The doors and windows are open. Fireworks sound in the distance. The night is close, intimate. Fleeting aromas of flowers mingle with pungent cigarette smoke. Cats, some stray, come and go then tarry as the meal is served. Scallops, duck confit, mache. A long languid evening sustained by bottles of earthy wine and tales of the Algerian War (Jean-Pierre fought in the war) and Bernadette's 83-year-old mother ("Mamita").

I learn when I phone my father to wish him happy birthday that my Aunt Virginia has died. She was the quietest of my mother's sisters. She was 85. Dad is flustered because he can't find his tax returns in the masses of boxes in his new house.

Sheets of rain, evanescent ghostly robes, sweep through the valley. A quick parade that leaves a freshness in the air smelling of grass and metal. A hawk lifts into a now blue sky, glides effortlessly before the vast sea, dipping, riding. It's the lightness, the being carried. This is freedom to me. Drifting out of earshot, preying on earth's beauty with a kestrel eye.

Bruce Chatwin's letters are almost better than his books. Less clipped, more revealing. I'm reading Nicholas Shakespeare's biography of Chatwin. I jot down in my notebook excerpts from letters Chatwin wrote about a "writer's paradise" in India, where he stayed with his wife Elizabeth while he worked on *The Songlines*.

*I adore it here. Lunch yesterday, for example, consisted of a
light little bustard curry, a purée of peas, another of aubergine
and coriander, yoghurt, and a kind of wholemeal bread the size
of a potato and baked in ashes. A sadhu with knotted beard
down to his knees has occupied the shrine a stone's throw from
my balcony; and after a few puffs of his ganja I found myself
reciting, in Sanskrit, some stanzas of the Bhagavad Gita. I
work away for eight hours at a stretch, go for cycle rides in the
cool of the evening, and come back to Proust.*

Today, in sorry defense of my harvest of rocks lugged
to the villa from Grand Fond, I read to Wendy from the
book on Chatwin:

*. . .Bruce liked to think of himself as someone who travelled
light, with only a brown leather rucksack. Made for him by a
saddler in Cirencester, this was a copy of a rucksack belonging
to the French actor Jean-Louis Barrault, whom Bruce had
sat next to on a plane. . .traveling with Bruce in India was
"like travelling with Garbo." Bruce's luggage included 40 kilos
excess baggage in books. There was also the typewriter, the card
index, the Champagne, the
muesli, the pills, the hats,
the boots, the grey suits,
the pyjamas.*

"You have 40 kilos of
rocks! They won't fit in a
leather rucksack."
  "I have a backpack,
not a rucksack."
  "You're not Garbo.
Well, maybe you are."

Randy and Maya come for lunch. They marvel at the view. "Our house is just below in the valley." Randy takes out his camera. Wendy serves quiche tarts and tabouli salad.

"Sorry I have to leave so soon." Randy stands up. "Have to set the tables."

Maya laughs. She stays well into the afternoon talking about island life, the lack of poverty, the possibility that it will all be spoiled by overcrowding and overdevelopment.

"I love this arrangement."

"Just things I found in the garden. Grasses, seeds, weeds."

Wind rattles the windows. Roosters and peacocks cry out. The view of green hills and blue sea is like a drug. "I could sit up here forever."

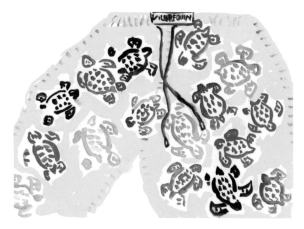

We meet Jean-Pierre at La Mandala for drinks. A wash of Matissean pink appears under the clouds over the harbor. Jean-Pierre talks freely about his past. He sailed from France to Mauritania when he thought he had six months to live. "My Labrador jumped off the boat near Corsica to swim with the dolphins." His mother died in Paris at the end of the war "after being bitten by a rat."

"Did you and Bernadette really win a dance contest?"

"That's when our romance began."

The old nudists at Gouverneur are gathered beneath their beach umbrellas like a pride of ancient lions under savannah trees. The wind kicks in, the umbrellas are lowered. Skinny prepubescent girls run ahead of the racing tide. A man in a red thong dashes headlong into the surf. The beach is under siege. Waves invade the bay like D-Day marines. Sand pelts the skin. "Mozart was a manic-depressive." Wendy looks up from her book, Peter Gay's biography of the composer.

"How many books have you read?"

"Six maybe. I can't read in this wind." She looks at me. "Your clavicle is really brown."

"It's my best part."

"Shall we go?"

"After a swim."

Slowly, rhythmically, with the patience of a bear fording a heavy stream, I churn through the choppy water.

I've learned to do this over time. When I was young I
swam as fast as I could 10 or 15 strokes without taking
a breath, thinking I was in a 50-meter Olympic race.
Now I swim longer distances in good if plodding form,
breathing regularly, calmly, under control. I swim blindly,
eyes closed, unafraid of what's in front of me or below. I
am pleasantly surprised at how this Zen-like approach has
developed organically over the years. Swimming toward
wisdom. Or maybe away from foolishness? Toward mellow
away from callow.

David and Sarah arrive. We open a bottle of
Champagne and sit on the long tiled veranda. The moon
rises in the purpling sky.

"A full moon in your honor," I say to Sarah. "Chin-chin."
"It's so yellow."
"You're so radiant," Wendy tells Sarah. "Like the moon."
"And bubbly, like Champagne."
David is full of talk about art school and New York.
"I have my own studio. On 14th Street. Richard Tuttle is
coming to critique our work."

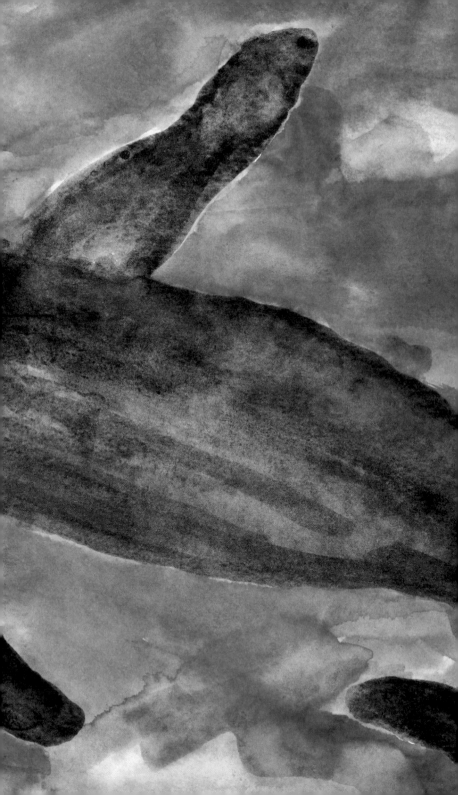

We drive down the mountain. The moon turns white, the sky indigo. Maya and Randy greet David and Sarah warmly. The restaurant is full as usual. It's true, Maya's is a place to be seen, as Jean-Pierre says. There are the elegant and the chic, dressed to impress. There are those dressed simply but nicely, sometimes loudly. Distinguished elders are here, usually with children and grandchildren. Americans, many Americans. Some Europeans.

There are a few who are famous, some so discreet as to be unnoticed, some discreet but always noticed. Many people know each other; greetings are exchanged cheerily and roundly as at a private club. The mostly French staff is young and attractive and friendly. The atmosphere is casual but classy, stylish but not stuffy.

Randy manages, Maya cooks. You can see her in the kitchen in her chef's whites. Both circle the tables, welcoming, kissing cheeks, giving the place a personal stamp. "What's bo bun?" Sarah asks, looking up from the menu.

"Vietnamese salad," Randy says. "Stir-fried with beef, vermicelli noodles, lemon grass, peanuts, shallots."

"Is it spicy? I like spicy."

High spirits aren't on the menu, but the airy island night brings them on. David and Sarah are in excellent form. "Dad thinks we're funny," Sarah says.

David retells the story of getting sick in a provincial restaurant in France when he was six. "We didn't know it was horse meat," I say.

"It was tongue," Wendy says.

"What's the difference?"

"Remember our first night in France in the Champagne region. We sat at a big round table in that fancy château. Mom, you were nervous because you couldn't reach us. You ordered one steak for David and me."

"*Un pour les deux.* How could I forget? Our first meal in France."

"Can you believe we traveled for six weeks that first trip? 1982."

"You were only three, Sarah."

"I remember Isabelle calling down from the tower at Bazouges. We were standing at the gate like beggars."

"And Madame Serrand wearing her pearls at the town swimming pool."

"Watching the village fireworks with Dominique on the bridge."

"Sarah wearing Isabelle's and Caroline's childhood dresses."

"Playing ping-pong with Eustache. And fishing in the river with Fred."

"And the *fête* in the square with the band and all the lights strung up."

"And the whole Serrand family singing in the château. '*Il y a longtemps que je t'aime.*'"

Marc comes to clean the pool. He's thin and has pale eyes and a pale Creole pallor. He's a friendly man with something of the outcast about him. "*C'est le premier jour du printemps,*" he says. "First day of spring." He stands on the side of the pool, looking out at the sea. He pulls the vacuum across the bottom of the pool. "Will be beautiful. Hot." He wears long pants, a long-sleeved shirt.

By the end of the day, David's chest and forehead, despite repeated smearings, have gone from blotchy flamingo pink to not quite *langouste* red. "Is there anything higher than 50?"

"Clothes," Sarah says.

"I sympathize with the pool man."

"**B**en is thinking about running for attorney general," Nancy says.

"I would vote for you."

"I'm hosting a fundraiser for Tom Daschle. I'll send you an invitation."

"Could you sleep in a room with a lizard?" Nancy asks Sarah.

Alain, the island photographer, stops by our table and, smiling, points to his camera. "Sure, why not?" We gather close and grin. Alain clicks away. He gives Ben his card.

"Demain après-midi." Alain flashes a pretty good smile himself. *"Mon studio à Gustavia."*

Suddenly the table is filled with desserts. "Did we order these?" Sarah asks.

"On the house." The waiter purses his lips.

"Oh, thank you, Thierry," Nancy says. "That's so nice."

Thierry blows her a kiss. *"De rien, ma cherie."*

"What are you doing later on tonight?"

"I'm sorry, Ben asked me first."

David and I drive to Grand Fond and hike along the bluff. We clamber along the trail past giant boulders and stands of wildflower. Frigatebirds glide in the cloudless blue. Waves crash on the rocks below. Boys paddle surfboards in the treacherous water. A man and woman have maneuvered their way down between the boulders and

David Au Grand Fond

drop-offs to lounge in shallow natural pools.

Every now and then the trail veers a little too close
to the edge. *"Faites attention."* David treads nimbly up ahead.
Young goats bleat as they follow their elders to higher
ground. French hikers in heavy boots approach. We step
aside to let them pass. The hot sun feels good. Traversing
this wild remote hillside has a cleansing effect. The strong
wind, the roaring sea strip away your complicated city self.
In an elemental landscape you feel more charged, more vital.

We stop in St. Jean to pick up food for lunch. David
goes into Casa del Habano. He comes back with thick dark
cigars in a box. "I have a crush on Sabrina."

"Does she smoke cigars?"

"Of course. That's how she knows what's good."

Late afternoon, a cool, misty day. David and I high-
step into the chilly water. The sun is behind the hill. The
beach is empty except for a man reading next to a rather
grand *château du sable.* And a tall black-haired man who is
delicately sticking his big brown foot into the water. *"Vamos,
cariño,"* he says to a woman standing by the dunes.

"Está muy frío?" she asks. She sheds her pareo and, nude, strides theatrically to the water's edge. "It's too cold." She jumps on his back. *"Vaminos."* He runs down the beach carrying her piggyback. He turns and they tumble laughing and yelling into the surf.

Christophe, the surfer, comes for lunch. He brings flowers for Sarah. He has glacial blue eyes and a scruffy beard. His long blond hair is wet and pulled back over his ears. *"Il y avait un requin près du Public,"* he says. *"Quatre mètres.* A shark. Four meters."

"Man-eating?" Sarah asks.

"Did you see it?"

"A friend told me."

It's a *Chacha la vie* lunch, lots of laughter. Christophe talks about his family in France. "Your family has a good time together. Mine is too formal."

"We're on holiday."

"I don't go on holiday with my family."

New
Dress

Wendy "Sarah Bernadette" "Les Jolies Boucles"

Lights blink in the houses across the valley, stars sparkle faintly. The idle hours before dinner. David studies his box of cigars. I have a glass of rum. A moth burns in the lamp, cicadas accompany Poulenc. Sarah appears in her new dress. "Dinner is two hours away," David says.

"I'm breaking it in."

"It's 55 degrees at home. No snow."

Moules night at La Marine. They are flown in from France. The diminutive sisters Anne and Isabelle scurry from table to table. Their family owns the popular quayside restaurant. Jean-Pierre sits between Wendy and Sarah, Bernadette between David and me. It's an intimate sextet.

"Verdine comes to our house every day at noon," Jean-Pierre says. "I feed her bananas so she won't eat the hibiscus." He puts one hand in front of the other, imitating the iguana's maladroit walk.

"Verdine?"

"I rub her neck."

"Bon soir."

"Bon soir, Anne. Ça va?" Jean-Pierre stands and kisses her on both cheeks.

"Busy, busy. *Et vous, ça va?"*

"*Ça va bien*," Bernadette says.

Jean-Pierre orders a Scotch "*avec trois glaçons.*"

The table fills with mussels and fries, cold shrimp and mayonnaise, *langouste* and sole, bottles of Chablis and water. "I went to Le Petit Club last night," Sarah says, "with my friend Christophe." Blond ringlets dance around her face, reddened by a day of sun. "It's definitely *petit.*"

"They try to make it feel bigger with all the mirrors." Bernadette has a bright smile, and also a bonnet of springy curls. "You look so much like your mother. With your beautiful curls."

"You have beautiful curls," Wendy says.

"Here's to the ladies and their beautiful curls." Jean-Pierre lifts his glass. "*Les boucles.*"

"*Aux jolies boucles.* Or is it *aux boucles jolies?*"

"Shall we speak French?" Bernadette says to David. "You studied in Paris, yes?"

Emboldened by Bernadette and the wine, David's French picks up. We all join in. Our comical pastiche of the two languages doesn't hinder communication. It's a lively dinner with nary a breath taken.

"No room for dessert."

"*Ah bah oui,*" Jean-Pierre says. "You must have *les crêpes au sucre. C'est la tradition.*"

"I've got to go." Sarah stands and gives kisses all around. "*Bonne nuit. À bientôt.* It was really fun."

"Be careful," I say.

"She's going to meet Christophe," Wendy says. "Moonstruck."

"*Qu'est-ce que c'est* moonstruck?" Jean-Pierre asks, pulling on his cigarette.

"*Un coup de foudre?*" Bernadette says. "Love at first sight."

"*Oui, un coup de foudre.*"

A strong wind puts the sea in a boil. Boats from Gustavia harbor seek refuge in St. Jean Bay on the other side of the island. A sailboat washes up on the beach near Maya's. This is the day we charter Pierre and his son Fabrice to take us sailing. "Rare for wind to come from southwest," Pierre says as we set off around the island on their 30-foot monohull. "Usually comes from east or southeast."

Sarah, worried about *mal de mer,* stays behind and makes a date for lunch with Christophe. We snorkel in the rain. When the rain picks up we retreat to the cabin for lunch. Pierre passes around homemade Planter's Punch. He tells us he and his family picked up sticks in Marseilles a few years ago and moved to St. Barts. "We may go back, but we're happy now."

"Sailing is for those who like to sleep," Fabrice says. "Just put the boat on autopilot and close your eyes." We don slickers and climb back outside. A big turtle paddles by. The rough sea makes us feel nervy and nervous.

"Why are there no other boats out?" David asks.

Pierre gives me the wheel. *"Comme une voiture."* Fabrice yanks it back when a sudden gust tips the boat a little too far. We motor the rest of the way back and are soaking wet when we pull into the harbor. Sarah is standing on the dock.

"I was getting afraid."

Our last night, dinner at Maya's. Gentle teasing of Sarah about her crush on Christophe. "Seasick, lovesick."

"The dishwasher thinks you look like an actor," the waiter says to David.

"Dad, you always fell asleep when you read to us at night. In mid-sentence."

"What was the name of the book, David, that you knew so well by heart."

"The Tyger Voyage."

"One night, you were about three, you starting reciting lines. You couldn't read yet."

"My father's got some curious friends./I guess I suppose it all depends/On what you mean by curious/But some are most unlike us."

"True, I do have some curious friends."

"Mom, you know a lot of Beatrix Potter."

"Not now."

"How about Ogden Nash?"

"Behold the duck./It does not cluck./A cluck it lacks./It quacks./It is specially fond/Of a puddle or pond./When it dines or sups,/It bottoms ups."

We laugh. "What's the other one?"

"'Very Like a Whale?'"

"Yes."

"'One thing that literature would be greatly better for/Would be a restricted employment by the authors of simile and metaphor.' And da-da-da-da-da-da... I can't remember."

"You remember the end..."

That's the kind of thing that's being done all the time by poets,
from Homer to Tennyson;
They're aways comparing ladies to lilies and veal to venison,
And they say things like the snow is a white blanket
after a winter storm.

Oh it is, is it, all right then, you sleep under a six-inch blanket
of snow and I'll sleep under a half-inch blank of unpoetical
blanket material and we'll see which one keeps warm,
And after that maybe you'll begin to comprehend dimly
What I mean by too much metaphor and simile.

Sarah is near tears. Christophe is not at the airport
to see her off. We wave at the little plane from the bar.
Christophe runs up just as it takes off.

 After lunch, Wendy and I head to St. Martin in a
chartered plane. "I see a whale."

 The pilot circles back for a closer look. "There!" The
whale leaps and turns over. The splash is tremendous, its
huge white belly like a floating cloud.

 "Kid in a pool," I say.

LA PLAGE

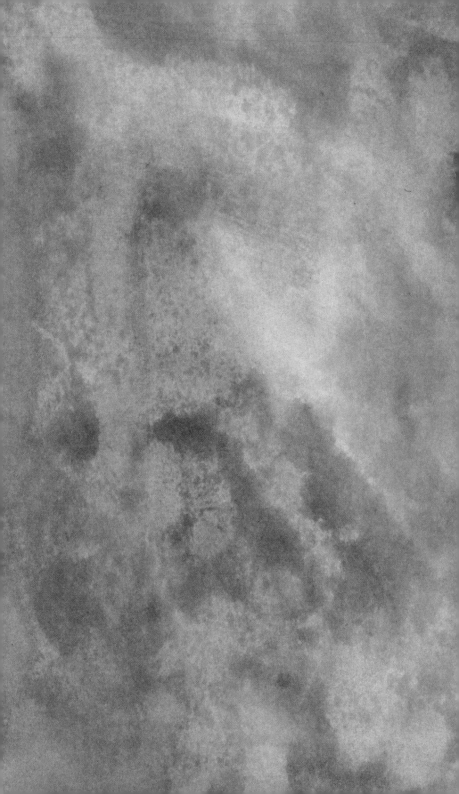

SIX

Beach Soccer

We fly in a weather-beaten chartered plane from Puerto Rico to St. Barts.

The name of the charter company is Air Mango. Larry Gray, the big-bellied pilot, greets us at the San Juan airport in shorts and T-shirt. Larry is also owner and porter. He takes our bags. "We have to hurry. St. Barts airport closes in a couple of hours. Can't land at night. No lights."

"He's like a bush pilot," Wendy whispers. Once airborne, Larry chats for awhile then pulls out his checkbook. He looks up now and then from paying bills to make sure all is clear. We approach St. Barts in clouds and rain and a slight sweat, at least I am. Above the island the clouds break. We descend through the shimmering arc of a rainbow as if through a gate.

"Welcome to paradise," Larry says on the ground. "No extra charge for the rainbow."

2002. A new house, this our ninth year. It's a few miles up the valley from St. Jean. It has a view of the airport, the pond, and hills cascading down to the sea.

Alas, no view of the sea. Roger and Catharine no longer rent Villa Lassus. We can see it, not without regret, high up on the mountain.

A cat meows in the kitchen. *"Mocha est triste,"* Jaquelyn, the caretaker, tells us. "He misses the owner." The owner's tropical paintings cover the walls. Bougainvillea blossoms dot the surface of the pool. A gentle wind blows through the valley as we have lunch on the porch. Doves coo, sugarbirds flit in the thick bushes. We may be a little *triste,* too, but not really. The sun is above us, the sea, healing as ever, is just over the hill. Also Maya's To Go has opened.

David takes an early morning flight from New York and is on Gouverneur beach in the afternoon. He has long hair and sideburns. With an MFA from Parsons, he is making his first forays into the art world. He sees a lot of the artist Duncan Hannah and his partner, the designer Megan Wilson. Duncan, a Minneapolis native and long-time New Yorker, has become a sort of mentor to David. "Funny that you've become friends with Duncan. He's the uncle of two of your earliest childhood friends."

"Who lived next door."

"Hannah and Sage," David says. "He was their Uncle Dunc."

quail eggs

Sarah pirouettes around the pool, long curls flying.

145

She's staying at a friend's house, and like David here only
for a few days. She goes out every night with island friends.
"What's for lunch?"

"*Wakame,*" Wendy says. I got it at Maya's To Go. It's
delicious. I had some this morning."

"Lots of iodine. Good for you."

"Something that green has to be good for you."

"We're also having quinoa salad and Creole
cucumber salad."

"All from Maya's To Go?"

"Yes."

"Beside salads?" I ask.

"Salmon sandwiches and quail eggs."

"I just remembered I'm meeting a friend for lunch."
Sarah jumps into the pool. "Just kidding," she says when
she surfaces. "I love seaweed."

An image of Sarah: beautiful in jeans and shimmering blouse, elbows on the table, cigarette and glass of wine in one hand. She's talking about a minor social scandal on the island. "Then she started going out with her friend's father…"

One pop, then another. "Hey, two with one swing!" Wendy is quite adept at zapping. She keeps the pink racquet close at hand while she reads. When you press the button, the electrified mesh is a lethal weapon (no permit required).

"Less wind, *plus de moustiques.*"

"A new racquet sport."

"A lot easier than tennis."

Pop.

Pleasure and pain, laughter and tears. They commingle on the island as they do everywhere. Life's surreal two-sidedness is ever-present, like an article in the paper about a bombing on one side of the page, an ad for an expensive necklace on the other. With one friend we talk about a child's marriage and their wonderful villa. With another, we discuss the prospect of the U.S. invading Iraq. From Randy and Maya comes the painful news that their son, Nicolas, almost died in a motorcycle accident.

"Bernadette is in Guadeloupe for a few days." Jean-Pierre stands in the small kitchen, making *canard aux navés.* Cats pad about. The veranda is a jungle of vines and branches. The jasmine has already bloomed, but the fragrance still hangs in the air. "We are thinking of moving back to France. I'm getting older. We can't afford a house on the island." A woman who just moved to St. Barts from

the Alps joins us for dinner. "The mountains are like the sea," she says.

A typical island dinner. Outdoors, breeze, wine, good food, cigarettes, talk. Talk about roots, provisional life, the fantasy of St. Barts, the cost of living, of families. About a sloth covered in moss in Costa Rica, the fauvists in Collioure. "He's a little bit of magic," Wendy says as we drive back on the dark roads.

Driving on the island with its narrow winding roads can be nerve-racking. Drivers are mostly polite, but with so many blind spots, slow trucks and fast motorbikes, and those who don't know their way, it gets a little dicey. Wendy holds on tightly to the door in the firm belief this will keep us safe. So far, save for a few bumps and scrapes, it has. "Thank god for the grip," I say.

Lunch at Le Tamarin (with newly fledged offspring).

"Who do you like better, Stephen Merritt or Rufus Wainwright?"

"Stephen Merritt. He's like Cole Porter. Great songwriter."

"Rufus is a better singer. And sexier."

"Both gay."

"Do you like Anne or Berenger?"

"Both."

"Berenger is sexier."

"Toothier."

"Dickens or Austen?" I ask.

At that moment Berenger strolls seductively among the tables, modeling a gauzy robe over a bikini. She stops at our table. "Sarah told me you have a diamond in your tooth," David says.

Berenger smiles and shows off the tiny white stone.

It has taken until middle age for me to dig into
"The Alexandria Quartet." Though some consider
Lawrence Durrell's writing elaborate and mannered, I
find it rich and lyrical. His tales of love in a hot climate,
and the changing narration, keep me turning pages.
From *Justine*, the first volume:

> *I stepped laughing out into the street once more to make a circle*
> *of the quarter which still hummed with the derisive, concrete life*
> *of men and women. The rain had stopped and the damp ground*
> *exhaled the tormenting lovely scent of clay, bodies and stale jasmine.*
> *I began. . .to describe to myself in words this whole quarter*
> *of Alexandria for I knew that soon it would be forgotten and*
> *revisited only by those whose memories had been appropriated by the*
> *fevered city, clinging to the minds of old men like traces of perfume*
> *upon a sleeve: Alexandria, the capital of Memory.*

We move to a villa in Pointe-Milou, on the other side
of the island. Sculpted islands, staggered like a stage set, jut
up across the water. In the distance is St. Martin, pale and
long as an odalisque in her bath. Narrow sweeping beaches

wrap around the bays of Lorient, St. Jean, and Flamands.
Backlit at sunset, the islands are fantastical silhouettes. The
sky above the graying sea is pastels of rose, lemon, and
apricot, like samples of makeup on a woman's cheek.

The house is rather suburban as is Pointe-Milou itself.
It's an actual neighborhood with streets of modern houses
and pools. The garden is large and lush with palm trees
lining a steep path to a diamond-shaped pool above the
crashing surf of the bay.

"I feel like I'm in Florida," Wendy says as she unpacks.

"Does looking at sunsets lower your IQ?"

"I prefer our rustic house on the other side."

We drape sarongs over the television. Wendy fills vases
with flowers. "The air conditioning means we won't have to
worry about mosquitoes."

"The view is spectacular. And the garden. We'll be fine."

We wake up the next morning to the sound of
hammers and saws and men speaking Portuguese. I look
over the fence at the neighboring house. A backhoe hovers
over a deep gash in the ground. *"Bom dia,"* one of the men
says. "Sorry for the bang-banging."

A hummingbird sits on a branch as we have breakfast. Its green tail is still for the moment, its small black breast glistening in the sun. Two military jets flash by barely above the water. Their metal sheaths flash like mirrors. The sound is deafening, the display of power chilling. Leonardo designed flying machines based on his studies of birds. Logical. He also designed weapons. It took centuries for man to fly and for planes to become weapons. Logic, fatal logic, made it inevitable.

A French journalist is writing a book claiming no plane crashed into the Pentagon in last September's terrorist attacks. The explosion was created by a bomb planted by the CIA, which provided reason for the U.S. to launch an attack on Iraq. We hear this from Jean-Pierre.

"Do you believe it?" I ask.

Jean-Pierre shrugs. "I don't know what to believe."

"Do you think that it really could have happened?"

"C'est possible."

Our annual lunch with Randy and Maya is at La Bête à Zailes. Jean-Marc, the owner, has a long ponytail and a winning smile. "How about a Mojito?" he says. He talks shop with Randy and Maya. "Business is good, yeah."

We order roulades of tuna and a bottle of rosé. "I'm reading *Salt*," Maya says.

"A 500-page book on salt." Randy smiles. "Can you imagine?"

"When did they stop mining salt on the island?"

"Back in the '50s, I think. People actually made a little money at it."

"It was impossible to make money before tourism."

"The beach at Saline was named after the salt marshes."

"Now money is made from Saline. It's the nicest beach

on the island."

"Saline solution," I say.

Dragon fruit appears on our dessert plate: slices
of white flesh speckled with black seeds inside a brilliant
crimson skin. The waiter brings the whole fruit, about the
size of an apple, to the
table. "16 dollars," he
says. "Grows on cactus."
Green petals protrude
from the red skin.

"Where is it from?
Wendy asks.

"South America."

"Amazing color."

"It's delicious."

"Kiwi in drag."

We go with Maya to Key West, a small club where
an American band plays. A large woman in a knit hat sits
on a stool and belts out songs to an enthusiastic crowd.
The dance floor is full. The room is hot. Jean-Pierre joins
us. *"Mon pieds sont…"* He starts to dance in place. *"Agités."*
The next thing we know he is on the floor dancing with an
enticing woman with dreadlocks.

"ZaZa," Maya says. "The sister of Yannick Noah."

"War clouds," Wendy says of the heavy gray masses
rolling over the island. They are gone by sunset and the sky
is a pale sheet of mango and peach. From the garden wall,
we watch surfers zig and zag in the breaking waves. It's the
vernal equinox. The sun is directly over the equator. Day
and night are equal. The waves seem higher. The light of

the soccer field offers faint echo to the strong light of the half moon. Lights from small planes flicker in the distance. Night closes in. Other than the muted crashing of the waves frogsong is the only sound.

At Maya's we say goodbye to Susan, the restaurant's longtime hostess and *"fille Vendredi."* A charming, down-to-earth English woman, she manages diners and tables with the aplomb of a field marshal in battle. She's leaving to start a bookstore.

"We'll miss you."

"I'll see you at my new shop."

"From menus to books."

"Bonne chance."

"Thank you. Hope people like to read half as much as they like to eat."

The long flight home. Sea gives way to land, to heartland towns lit in darkness. Ahead the fading gray, behind the indelible blues.

SEVEN

Villa Au Petit Pont

It is the breezes as much as the blues.

It is the sun that you somehow forgot is hot, it is the
first plunge, the cooing doves, the sailboats. It is the shock
of color, the glass of rum, the grilled fish. These things that
you know, you know again, pleasures that you love, you love
again. Fresh again, they refresh you. They are part of the
fabric, the warp and weft, of your life.

Villa au Petit Pont, high up on Lurin, has a sweeping
view. To the north and west is the harbor, the hills of
Colombier, and St. Martin in the distance. To the east is St.
Jean Bay and Eden Rock, and the trio of deserted islands—
Île Frégate, Île Chevreau, and Île Toc Verts. Beyond is the
Atlantic. In the foreground to the west is the ruin. A hotel
shattered by Hurricane Luis seven or eight years ago, it sits
high on a rocky cliff, wrapped in vines, windows blown out,
hawks surveying from rotting porch railings.

In front of the house is a big garden spanned in the
middle by a small arched bridge. Every other day, Raphael,
a silent ageless man in straw hat, shorts, and sandals, waters

the many flowers—bougainvillea, frangipani, allamanda, jasmine, hibiscus. The house is roomy and airy with big

windows open at every turn to sea, garden, sky. Ana is the housekeeper (she told us about the house). It's good to have her with us again, her easy smile, her gentle, playful manner. She, Yves, and Lucas live in a tiny house up the hill.

Mornings reading by the pool, lunches on the porch, afternoons swimming in the sea, after-dinner strolls along the harbor. Paradise, yes. Well, not quite. Upstairs in the villa is a television. CNN broadcasts 24 hours a day America's invasion of Iraq. It's March 2003.

Saturday. Planes drop from the west over the hillside onto the little airstrip or hop up into the eastern sky above the beach. A plane landing from the east (a rarity) pulls up suddenly as another descends rapidly from the other direction. Yachts pass, headed for Gustavia or a protected cove. Giant cruise ships and elegant sailboats are parked in the harbor.

We have drinks on the porch and watch the sun set.

Strings of lights on the ship masts shine in the pink-blue sky. They make up somewhat for the gracelessness of the boats. When one ship leaves the harbor, three old-fashioned horn blasts roll across the hills. Night falls. The coastline and the hills and the big rock guarding the port fade to black. Something both expectant and melancholy rides the soft tropical air. Peacefulness tinged with vulnerability, even unease. The ruin bereft of color, of purpose, looks beautiful but forlorn.

St. Martin is a pale gray strip beneath a cloud the shape of a dragon. A final plane lands. That seems the signal for crickets and frogs to start up. Lights on the soccer field come on, and in the harbor and the houses across the hills. Headlights appear on the winding roads, in the violet sky, early stars.

In the shade of an ancient flamboyant tree, we gather one Sunday at a long clothed table. Ana, Yves, and Lucas and their friends (who live near us)—the robust, gray-haired François (*née* Francisco in Spain), his young Breton wife Natalie, their tall skinny son Jean, and Jean's girlfriend Emmanuelle. The table is filled with quiche, grilled sausage, salad, cake. Also ceviche of bonita and wahoo, compliments of François, who hauled the fish out of the sea yesterday. A standing army of wine.

Conversation is in French, ours rough but tolerated. This a rare case of our French being better than their English. François, a gregarious voluptuary, drinks Diet Coke. "Doctor's orders." He talks longingly of vintage wines. A building contractor, now retired, he lives near Versailles. He tells us that he once worked for Fernand Léger and refused as payment one of Léger's paintings. *"Je voulais de l'argent,"* he says. "Not so smart, eh?"

We talk about life on the island and about the unification of Europe but strangely not about the war. We talk about American actors. "I love American actors," François says. "Clark Gable."

"Harrison Ford," Natalie says.

We take turns singing songs from our youth. We all applaud after François sings. He has a marvelous voice. He sings or hums as he grills or goes to the kitchen. The sun sets. Seven hours after breaking bread under the big tree, Wendy and I walk back to the villa, picking our way in the clinging night behind the weak beam of *une lampe de poche.*

Wendy goes upstairs every day to "check on the war." CNN reports on the march to Baghdad. "American forces are 50 miles away." Scenes of protest in the Arab world and in the U.S. We protest the war, but like most we feel helpless and, here on this beautiful island, a little silly and superfluous. We worry about possible terrorist attacks in New York, where David and Sarah are now both living. We are not comforted to hear that helicopters are circling the city on the lookout.

I'm reading *Shroud* by John Banville, another marvelous British writer. Among many wonderful passages in the book is this about wartime London:

> The city was all plangent airs and melancholy graces. I am
> thinking of the rich, deep sheen on the casings of wooden
> wirelesses; of asthmatic taxis, black and square as hearses with
> crosses of black tape on their headlamps; of a certain dish of
> quails' eggs, washed down with mugs of woody-tasting tea,
> eaten late at night in a strange bed in someone's flat somewhere;
> of loud singing in low places; of Laura's hand on my wrist

as she turned laughing at some joke and caught my eye and let
the laugh turn into a look of love and longing that was no less
affecting for being almost entirely fake.

A large turtle, the size of a soccer ball, ambles into
the garden. Patches of amber mark the dark hexagons on
its shell. Scales on its long swiveling neck and stout legs are
bright orange. Wendy picks up a blossom and holds it out.
The turtle takes the flower under its horned beak. It drinks
greedily from the cup of water Ana puts out.

"It's not afraid," Wendy says.

"Il a faim."

Hawks swoop between the palms along the pool.
Doves converse in the thickets, sugarbirds chase. A small
finch-like bird with a reddish throat pecks at crumbs on the
patio table then sails into the kitchen as if invited for lunch.
Hummingbirds work over the garden's flowering bushes.
Frigatebirds and pelicans ride the drafts not far above.

"This house is for the birds," I say to Wendy as we sit
by the pool. "Literally. They're everywhere."

"You must be happy."

I climb the stairs to the patio. In the kitchen, battalions
of ants, the size of pinheads, swarm over a dead moth.

Funny Face is the name of Susan's bookstore. It's on
the second floor of the old Creole building in the center of
town, above Alma, the venerable dry-goods store. Windows
and porch look out at the big flamboyant tree in the
courtyard of Le Select. It has a good but limited selection
of French and English titles. There are small reading rooms
for children and a sitting room where you can eat cakes and
drink tea. We are the only ones in the shop.

Susan wonders if she can make it work. "I have to sell

books at a higher price than in the U.S. or France."

"It's so nice to have a bookstore like this on the island."

"That's what I thought," Susan says and smiles. "Could be just a pipe dream."

We say goodbye and go down the stairs to the street. Le Select is full. The air smells of fried hamburgers. "Three more books to add to the pile," Wendy says.

"Have to help out. You need more books to read. You'll enjoy *Le Rouge et Le Noir*. Ever read anything by Stendahl?"

"You didn't buy the French version?"

"There's a pretty good French/English dictionary in the villa. *Larousse.*"

David and Sarah arrive together from New York. Ana fills the house with flowers. They share a bedroom with big windows looking out at sea and hills and boat-filled harbor. We have dinner at Maya's. "You brought the rain," Randy tells them. "It hasn't rained in months. We're very happy to see you."

The villa cisterns fill up, the small lime tree in the garden springs back to life. Raphael relaxes a little. We are mildly upset that he has been drastically pruning the trees and flowers. He cuts according to the moon, Ana tells us.

David and Sarah drive to town to buy salads and tarts and wines. I remember in earlier years Sarah clamoring for fresh *pain au chocolat*. I had to drive down to the bakery before breakfast. I'm glad to hand them the keys. *"Faites attention,"* I say.

David and I walk down the long road that leads to the ruin. It was a fancy hotel, a kind of compound with gardens sitting on a cliff overlooking the sea. A rusted car, tires shredded, wipers angled across the windshield, sits under a tree. We walk inside. Scattered around are chairs, dishes, books, waterlogged, tattered, broken. Collapsed walls, holes in the floor. A girl's faded blue dress hangs over the back of a chair. A chandelier lies on a moldy table. "Looks like they dropped everything and ran."

"This was a pretty nice place. They paid for the setting. Lots of atmosphere but not a lot of protection."

"Amazing it's still like this. It's been years since Luis."

Seeing this kind of destruction is perhaps more powerful than seeing the place as it was before the storm. The damaged is more evocative somehow than the undamaged. The wrecked hotel has a strange mesmerizing beauty, like a decaying Havana house in a Polidori photograph.

What happened? Were people here during the storm? Did they really flee? Why hasn't it been repaired or at least cleaned up? One can only imagine.

ruin

One night at L'Iguane, Sarah introduces us to Mario, the owner. Part Italian, part French, he has befriended Sarah over the years. He is a music impresario of sorts and talks about festivals on the island. "I met a guy from Pink Floyd on a yacht one year."

Mingling at the bar is a young couple who have boutiques on the island and in New York. "This is Jerome and Jenny." Also at the bar is Bobby, "the pirate," a dreadlocked, gaggle-toothed man from Guadeloupe who depends on friends for food and shelter. He walks each afternoon on Gouverneur with his German shepherd.

At dinner Sarah tells us she met Miki, the man who owns the big estate next to Gouverneur. "He made a fortune in some hi-tech business and now makes music with his band in the recording studio. It's on his property."

"Doesn't hang out with Bobby, the pirate, I suppose?" David says.

Waves break high on the beach. Small, black eyes stick out like periscopes in the sand. Crabs emerge and do their fleet soft shoe. An elderly woman walks straight into the sea without pause. She dives in straightaway and swims far out. She turns and swims slowly toward the rocks on the other side of the bay. Slowly, she swims back. This takes half an hour. She stops three or four times.

Boys ride boogie boards or run across the sand at full speed and hurl themselves into the water like running backs diving across the goal line. They smoke cigarettes, sitting on the sand soaking wet. A girl tenderly rubs lotion over her boyfriend's back.

Treading water, we look for goats on the hill. Mixes of white, black, and brown, they are well-camouflaged. When pickings are slim, they prop forelegs on branches and nibble on higher leaves. Single-minded as pilgrims, they wind nimbly through the rocks and bushes, in sight one moment, out of sight the next. I don't know if they find enough to eat, but they always find their way.

"Does Verdine still come here?" David asks.

"Every day for lunch," Bernadette says. *"Parfois avec un petit ami,* with a boyfriend. She comes when I call her."

Jean-Pierre pours more wine. Cats crisscross the porch, looking for handouts. "Are the cats afraid of Verdine?" Sarah asks. She gives Ballou, the biggest cat, a piece of bread.

"The cats stay out of her way."

"Ballou looks like a lynx," David says.

"I was going to do an internship at a hospital in Ho

Chi Minh City," Bernadette says. "I could not go because of SARS."

"It has not been a good year for my painting," Jean-Pierre says. "I had to leave my studio because there was so much noise from construction. I wrote a novel. It's going to be published."

"That's exciting," Wendy says. "Congratulations."

"What's the book about?" Sarah asks.

"It's called *La Vie à l'Envers*. It's about the life of a man told in reverse, from old age to childhood."

"Jean-Pierre goes to Kyoto in winter for an artist's residency. I want him to keep painting. Though it is nice he found a publisher for his book."

"People are not buying my work as much as before."

"Did you know Nureyev?" I ask.

"I remember him in his last years when he was sick, walking through town in a long scarf and sweater."

Sarah: "I didn't mean to stay out all night, but it was disco night. We dance and sweat half to death. Then we go out to the front and air out and have a coupe."

Wendy: "I like this writer. He's like me. He goes off track."

The garbage collector stops his truck in front of the fish market in Lorient. The day's catch, including giant *langoustes,* is spread across a table. The crusty fishmonger weighs six or seven daurade (sea bream) on his primitive scale and tosses them into a plastic bag. The garbage man runs back across the street with the bag, hops in his rig, and drives off. We watch this transaction from our car behind the truck on the island's main road. Traffic backs up but no one honks.

We pack to the sound of thunder. Lightning flashes above the sea. The storm breaks, knocking out windows and flooding the house. Sarah's suitcase is soaked. "Can I stay a few more days until my bag dries out?"

arm in

arm in arm

EIGHT

When I open my notebook, I find sand stuck to the pages and pale dried flowers.

My notes from last year are legible, the colors of watercolor and ink drawings still fresh. I find that I start my note-taking later each year, distracted, worried that I write the same things. Days and nights are pretty much the same, a lovely, blissful same.

This place is the same, Villa au Petit Pont. Same as it was last year. The house with the little bridge that crosses the lush garden of palms and flowers.

Ana is here, smiling and cheerful and fit. She hikes every day up the long steep hill from Gustavia. The first thing she does when she arrives is fill vases and bowls with flowers from the garden. Silent Raphael is here, minding the garden and pool and gazing out in what seems like mourning at the view.

The view is the same. Ships are in the harbor, small planes dip in and out of the sky, the ruin still stands on the hill to the west, looking more battered and picturesque. The islands are here, the wraparound ocean. The birds are here. Doves, sugarbirds, hawks, pelicans, frigatebirds. A black hummingbird with neon green crest hovers over the vase of flowers in the kitchen window. Yesterday on our way to St. Jean a dozen wild peacocks paraded across the road in front of our car.

In the larger world, volatile and frenetic, constancy is rare. Things change, and they should or will, but fundamentally the island is the same from year to year. This dreamy place will never be truly real, but the more we come, the more real it is. It gets better each year, richer, more textured in the way a good play does over the course of its run.

The island is a refuge, of course, an escape from winter, from the urban world. But more than running from something it's running to something. To the gentle breeze, the healing sea, the high blue sky. Simple natural things that are so profound, so necessary.

A storm pushes rain into the covered porch on the ocean side. High on Lurin, we are exposed to the elements. We sit on the garden porch and listen to the music of the rain. It has movements, like a concerto: soft (*piano*) for a while, loud (*forte*) for awhile, a beginning, a middle, an end.

Sarah and David are here, David with his *copine* Elizabeth, a bright, attractive woman who works in a museum in New York. David, sporting espadrilles and head scarf, remains an avid lover of books and lunch. This year, with a television in the house, he watches college basketball playoffs.

Sarah remains a worshipper of sun and dance. She eats shrimp, smokes, and romances a boy with a scooter and a tattoo. Wendy wraps a sarong around her head to protect against the sun. She reads constantly and relishes Maya's salads. She makes breakfast smoothies of banana and melon and complains that her chin is too sunburned. She talks to David about cooking.

I gather flowers from the garden floor, fallen hibiscus, allamanda, bougainvillea, the dead and dying ones. I spread them on the big dining room table to dry or put them in books and newspapers. I hope I can get them back to my studio. Can a customs dog sniff out hibiscus? "What are you going to do with them?" Wendy asks.

"You know, that thing."

"What thing?"

"You know, that
art thing."

At Gouverneur,
a young French boy
proudly carries a
shark's tooth to his
mother. Two studious-
looking American
teenagers, floating in shallow water, discuss American history. The boy rattles off the names of American wars. "When was the First World War?" he asks his sister.

A French woman plays with two young girls. She pulls off her daughter's swimsuit bottom and, teasingly holding it in the air, runs through the surf. A chubby Argentinian rides a buzzing jet ski back and forth from a yacht squatted like a warship in the bay.

A gracious white-haired woman (wearing a big straw hat and a respectable swimsuit) says to her nude husband, "Boy, the sun is hot."

"Sure is." He places his Green Bay Packers cap over *les bijoux de famille.*

We go one morning to Grand Fond. David and Elizabeth climb the bluff and hike the goat path above the crashing waves. Wendy and I comb the beach, rather comb the rocks on the beach. I fill my bag with the smooth gray rocks that look like they've been sculpted by Henry Moore.

We take the long way back to the villa, passing Nureyev's house and the luxury hotels (surprisingly unassuming), leaning into the corniche above Eden Rock. We crawl through the bustle of shops and scooters and jaywalking flesh in St. Jean.

"Time for lunch," David says as we pile out of the little Japanese wagon.

A four-masted schooner has pride of place in the turquoise harbor. Hawk chicks screech from their nest near the ruin, doves coo by the house. A breeze blows gray-white clouds from blue Atlantic sky to blue Caribbean sky. The table fills with wine and food. The view is part of the meal. An hour passes, another and another, in this heavenly lair, this "dream-cloud," as Durrell might say.

Yves comes each day to pick up Ana. He spent much of the winter in Guadeloupe receiving chemotherapy. His cancer is in remission. He tells us the mayor has put a temporary halt to building on the island. *"Les artisans n'ont pas de travail."* Yves is a small man with small feet and a mass of thick hair. Like Ana, he has a ready smile.

Son Lucas plays soccer and goes with his team on the ferry to play matches in St. Martin. He takes sailing lessons at school. Shy and pretty for a boy, he comes one afternoon to swim in the pool. *"Il n'aime pas à nager à la mer,"* Ana says.

The island is not all smoothie and bougainvillea. At Shell Beach one day Wendy steps on a sea urchin. The pharmacist gives her cream and tells her *la penne*, the quill, will work itself out.

Cactus thrives in the dry climate. Peruvian apple and prickly pear add spiky sculptural form to the soft flourish of hibiscus and oleander. The gray-green of the agave is a lovely color. I like the way the big fleshy leaves flop and twist like tongues or rabbit ears. At least until the wind blows my cap into the middle of a needly patch.

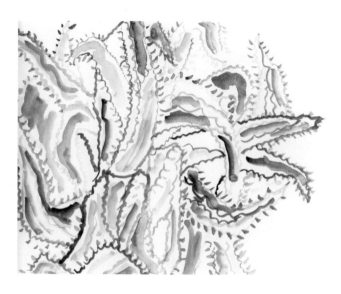

Jean-Marc also has a ready smile. We sit with him one night at his restaurant on the harbor beneath moon and stars. He talks about raising his young son on the island.

"It's a wonderful place to grow up, but there is no high school." He wonders if he will return with his family to France. We drink a glass of *rhum vanille* and take our nightly stroll through the port. Town kids sit on scooters and smoke and listen to hip-hop, meters from couples chattering over dinner on their rented yachts with uniformed crews and big-screen TVs.

"Cheers."

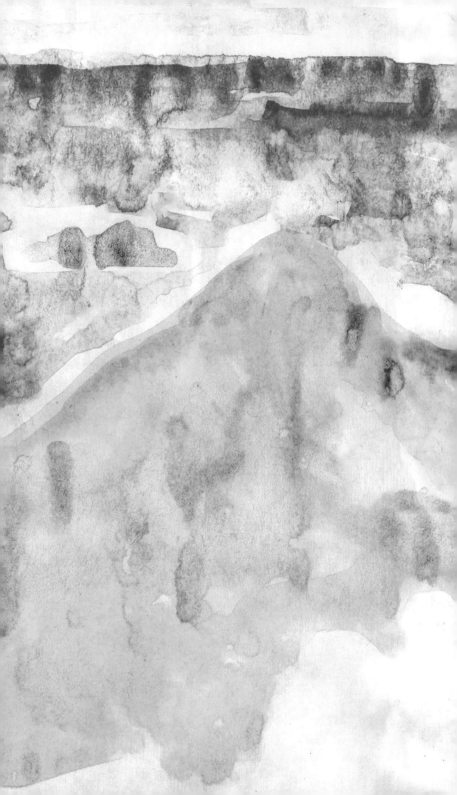

We look for planets in the evening sky. "You can see five," Elizabeth says. She has a map. We find Venus, Jupiter, Mars, Saturn. Stars mingle with the planets.

"Is Jupiter the largest planet? Or is it Saturn?"

"Which one has the red spot?"

"Jupiter."

"That's the largest."

"Saturn has rings."

"What are the rings made of?"

"Gas. I think the planet is mostly gas."

"Find out a lot by looking at the heavens."

"Astronomy 101."

"Do you want to spend September in New York?" David asks at lunch. He's going to London to work as an intern for the magazine *Modern Painters*. He's excited but worries about subletting his New York apartment.

Sarah joins us. She's carrying a big helmet. "I went dancing with Maya last night. I couldn't keep up with her. She was wearing a J'adore Dior T-shirt and had red lips and danced like a wild woman."

Sunday morning. David, Wendy, and I walk along the
pond. Hordes of tiny crabs scurry around mud holes. Big
pelicans smash into the water like kamikazes, shorebirds
stalk quietly among the reeds: two different approaches
to life. At the archery field, a pair of lovers shoots arrows.
After each shot, they kiss then walk arm in arm to the
targets. At the newly painted firehouse, rowdy firemen sit
outside enjoying lunch.

Kiki, a German surfer, is the new hostess at Maya's.
"We always have a table for you, Mr. Coggins." She has
never lived longer than six months in any one place. She
goes in the off-season from island to island around the
world in search of waves.

Sebastien, a handsome waiter with a ponytail, chats
with Sarah. Tomato and mango salad is still on the menu,
so is grilled daurade with Creole sauce, and *gateau à l'orange*.
All hell would break loose if Maya's menu changed.

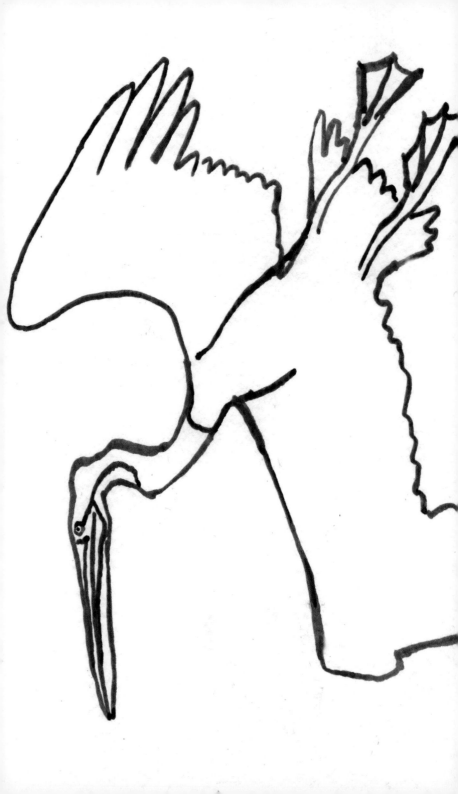

un ruban in les fois

un ruban dans ses cheveux

The Wall House is a new restaurant on the harbor across from the museum. Franck, the chef and owner, goes in his whites from table to table describing daily specials. Fellow owner Denys, short and fast-talking, carves lamb and duck roasted on the spit and poses for wine-loud Americans. David, a fan of grilled food, likes it here.

At lunch one day on the harbor, we see a small fishing boat pull up to the quay. A tan skinny man steps off. In each hand, he has a large *langouste*, glistening pink and white. He holds them by the antennae as he takes them into a restaurant.

"They're beautiful," Wendy says. "But I don't like to see them squirming."

"Wonder what he gets for them? If it's even half what they charge in the restaurant."

Another night we're at Eddy's. We're the last people there. "Want to see something nice?" Eddy asks. We follow him into the kitchen. On a counter is a big tuna, the skin a gleaming bright silver. "Yellow fin," Eddy says. A chef slices large filets of the dark red meat. The flesh is so fresh it seems to quiver.

"Did you just get it?"

"A fisherman brought it in a little while ago."

"It was just caught?"

"They fish at night."

Eddy looks at a clock on the wall. It's just after midnight.

"I'm reading *Don Quixote*," Randy announces at lunch.

"In Spanish?"

Maya talks about building on Nantucket, where Randy has property. "Would you leave St. Barts?"

"One day maybe."

"Are you optimistic about the future of the island?"

"People will keep coming."

"That's the problem. Too many people."

A man with a long ponytail gets up from his lunch at the bar and without warning bangs out a mournful tune on the piano. The sun is hot. We sit under an awning eating sushi and drinking sake.

"Have you seen the big yacht?" Randy asks. "It takes

up ten berths."

"It's tied parallel rather than perpendicular."

"Size of a small office building."

"A woman who lives in California charters it every year. She rents a villa so her children can play video games."

Jean-Pierre and Bernadette have moved to a house in Gustavia near Shell Beach. It's full of bamboo trees and bougainvillea and sugarbirds but is also oddly dark and airless. Bernadette's brother Olivier and his Japanese wife are visiting from Luxembourg. It's the last day of The Bucket. We've gathered for drinks.

Jean-Pierre has just come from a boat that was in the race. "We came in last. There was little wind. *Très, très chaud.* I must shower." He returns in a Vietnamese silk tunic and we sit at a long table in the garden, swatting mosquitoes and listening to Bernadette's stories of Vietnam. She was there over winter, learning about acupuncture.

"Two of my friends had acupuncture," Sarah says. "One it helped, the other it didn't. It just hurt."

Olivier is quite voluble. He voices his opinions snappily in fluent English: American films are too violent, cigarettes are terrible, bad email grammar is inexcusable. But he has brought a good bottle of red Bordeaux.

"We lived in Des Moines for awhile," Olivier's wife says.

"There was a lot of variety in the landscape," Olivier says. "On one side of the road, corn, on the other, soybeans."

Jean-Pierre chain-smokes. He tells us in his gravelly voice that his artist's residency in Kyoto is next winter. "I thought it was this winter. I did not look at the year," he says sheepishly. He was in Paris for the publication of his book. "It has sold thousands of copies." His second book has been accepted for publication and he's working on a third.

"What kind of art do you make?" Jean-Pierre asks David.

"It's kind of conceptual."

"Do you paint?"

"More a combination of photography and a kind of performance."

"Do your cats like your new house?" Wendy asks.

"Ballou likes it. Lots of mice," Bernadette looks beneath the table where the big cat is in fact toying with a live mouse. "But he is sick."

"C'est vrai?" Sarah says. *"Il n'est pas bien? Pauvre Ballou, pauvre chat. Quel est le problème?"*

"Your French is good, Sarah," Bernadette says.

"She's been going to night school," David says.

"I go out at night with my French friends," Sarah says, laughing.

David's and Sarah's last night. We walk along the harbor under the full moon. Tied to the pier are the big sailboats here for the race. Some are over 50 meters long. They are lit up and lively with parties. Ropes creak, fish swim in the eerie underwater light. The names of the boats are less evocative than their places of registry: London, Cayman Islands, St. Tropez. On shore barefoot sailors, male and female, drink and woo.

"Would you like to charter a boat and sail the seven seas?"

"Sounds nice but too confining."

"I prefer *terra firma.*"

"A sailboat is a vessel of desire, of possibility."

"Expensive toys for pompous boys."

"Of romance, of freedom.

"Dad, you're a vessel of…"

"Don't say it. Claptrap and drivel?"

"I was thinking more twaddle and bunk…"

What is it about the beach that makes us happy? What is it about the sand and the waves? Because it returns us to childhood? We shed clothes in the presence of strangers. Shed our shackles, our burdened prosaic selves. We run and dive and splash in the water. We yell and whoop. We read and dream and jog and stroll. We drink and smoke and play games with friends and family. We embrace, we snooze

open-mouthed, we turn colors. We build castles, we bury ourselves. We do what we want, we are liberated. Kids again. All it takes is a beach.

Easter, our last day. Restaurants are closed. Cold *langouste* for lunch, rack of lamb for dinner. We swim in the sea in the afternoon and walk along the harbor after sunset. We drink rum while we wait for the lamb to warm up in the alien microwave.

We eat on the terrace beneath a starry sky. Frogs sing, crickets chirp. There's a breeze. "Is this is the first time we've had dinner in a villa not in a restaurant?" I ask. "After all these years."

"Do you think we should get a microwave?"

"If we had a house here we would eat at home most of the time."

"I'd have to cook," Wendy says. "I just saw a falling star."

"Isn't it a meteor not a star?"

"If I make a wish it will come true."

"What's your wish?"

"If I tell you it won't come true."

hermit crab

The Bucket

NINE

School kids roam the streets of Gustavia like cows in India.

Pale bodies from the cruise ships plod along the narrow sidewalks. Our plane from St. Martin just landed. After a stop at the grocery store it's up the hill to Villa au Petit Pont. It's a sunny afternoon in early March.

Ana is cleaning frantically. "Last people left an hour ago."

"How is your family?" Wendy asks. "How is the island?"

Lucas is fine, but Yves is in Guadeloupe recovering from an operation. Villa Lassus has been bought by an Italian family. The ruin has been bought by an American man. And sadly Jean-Pierre had an aneurysm and is in a Paris hospital. "We must call Bernadette," Wendy says.

"She is on the island," Ana says.

The villa has a fresh coat of paint. Must have been a sale on egg yolk yellow.

"*Au revoir à l'hiver,*" I say as I slip into the pool.

"The doves are welcoming us," Wendy says.

After dinner we walk through town. It's quiet except for one or two places where people drink and listen to a singer or a little reggae band. The smiling new moon is high in the sky. Twitching gently in the vast darkness above the villa are a million and one stars.

In the garden this morning two green lizards joust. They circle each other, spreading their chin fans. Finally one clamps on to the other's mouth in a kind of dragon's lip-lock. They thrash and pull while a brilliant hummingbird dips in the flowers around them. A variation of that scene is repeated at dinner.

At the table next to us are two cigars sticking out of a shirt pocket. Owner of the shirt and cigars is a white-haired New Yorker. To his friend who is of roughly the same vintage, he says, "It has to be at least 200 feet to get any respect."

"How much?" the friend asks.

"200 grand a week."

"200 grand?"

"Yeah, a 100 feet, a 100 grand."

The friend whistles and looks at the women at the table. "I'm in. How about you?"

"Maybe." The first man looks at the women at the table, their wives. "Whadaya think?" he says to them. He takes a cigar from his pocket. He smells it, studies it. "A lot for a week. Beaucoup."

The women are excited. Younger than their husbands, they are coiffed and chiseled. "It would be so much fun," one says.

"Monaco in the spring. Yes, please!" the other says.

The first man hands a cigar to his friend then strikes a match. "Of course I'm in." Flame shoots up, curling smoke. He grins. "Whadaya think?"

A lone soaring frigatebird in a Whistleresque gray sky above Saline. Frigatebirds stay aloft for weeks on wings that span seven feet.

Sea urchins on the rocks at Gouverneur, clinging black

pin cushions. Crabs, too, scuttling then clinging when waves
splash up.

The piercing whistles of tropicbirds as they circle the
cove. A tropicbird cannot walk because its feet are so far
back on its body.

A school of slender white fish in a curling wave.

A *tortue* feasting on fallen fruit on the villa road.

Two sea rays gliding elegantly along the shore at Eden
Rock, lit by underwater lights. Fluttering veils, they come
and go in seconds.

A wild goat, black and
brown like a saddle shoe,
grazes on the roadside above
Gouverneur. Spiraling horns,
stern eye. It stares at us.

Migrating humpbacks.
Over a thousand pass by the
island, including many young.
The tail of the whale is like a
fingerprint, unique and exclusive
to each.

A sugarbird flies from
garden to pool through the house. I stand in the dining
room with morning coffee. Birds often fly into the house.
This is the first time I have seen one fly *through*. Faster than
going around, I think, but a little risky.

The line between inside and outside blurs. Views
through the villa's big arched doors and windows are filled
with bursts of pink bougainvillea, green palm, blue sea,
and sky. Murmuring doves are the first thing we hear in the
morning, geckos clutch interior stucco walls, meals are eaten
outside or in open-air rooms.

A new villa today. Still in Lurin but closer to Gustavia.
Down a steep driveway just off the main road, it's a long,
open house set in the side of a steep hill thick with cactus
and *gaiac* trees. Just below is a small cove that opens to a
broad sweep of Caribbean. On the horizon is the island
of Saba, upright and pointed like a witch's hat. The house
faces west.

A large Buddha lords over the terrace, much of which
is covered and furnished with long sofas. As the sun sets
beyond the infinity pool and the sea, we light candles and
turn on the patterned Moroccan lamps. We drink rum by
the pool and feel, in this exotic spot, we have come to the
island for the first time.

"Let's call it *Villa d'Eau*," Wendy says. The big, blue-
tiled pool appears to flow into the sea. The sea is close.
We hear its incessant clatter and faint voices from sailboats
moored in the cove.

We could easily call the house Villa Outside-In or
Inside-Out. The line is blurred even more here. All rooms are
open to the wild. Gauzy nets drape the beds. Bougainvillea
blossoms whisk across the terra-cotta floors, like hot pink
crabs. Sugarbirds and lizards consider the place theirs. Goats
bleat in the dense woods across the gorge.

At Le Tamarin the house parrot flies in with a shriek to join the lunch crowd—clinging with sharp nimble claws to a chair back, eerily eyeballing us. I wonder if this is the same creature that terrorized us years ago. It tears at a crust of bread and poses for a few photos. It hooks a straw coaster as if a prize in its giant beak and flies back to its perch on the other side of the garden.

David arrives from New York in baseball cap and black and white tie. He piles his bag into the back of the car and we take the curving road up the mountain to the villa. Talk in the first 24 hours is non-stop, broken only by swimming and sleep. Over dinner at Wall House, on the walk along the harbor, at the villa under a bright moon, we talk. He is now a contributing editor to the British arts magazine *Modern Painters*. Several of his reviews have been published. He gives us his card. He goes to London often to visit Laura. "Last time I was there, we went to her

family's house in Wales."

Sarah is in Paris where she is studying fashion at Parsons School of Design. This is the first time she has not joined us in St. Barts. We don't feel too sorry for her because she is spending spring break with friends in the south of France. We miss her, as do many on the island. "Where is Sarah?" "Is Sarah coming?"

I am reading *The Master,* Colm Tóibín's beautifully written novel about Henry James. An excerpt:

> *And in one of those letters she had written the words which Gray had repeated to him and which Henry thought now maybe meant more to him than any others, including all the words he had written himself, or anyone else had written. Her words haunted him so that saying them now, whispering them in the silence of the night brought her exciting presence close to him. The words constituted one sentence. Minny had said, "You must tell me something that you are sure is true."*

New villa, old routine. Mornings reading, painting, sunning, swimming. Rose comes every day at lunchtime and bids us *"bonjour"* then *"bon appetit."* She brings flowers and chats with Wendy in French. A new wrinkle: the house has Wi-Fi. David breaks from books to check emails.

Afternoons for an hour or two *à la plage*, evenings reading, painting, enjoying sunset and moonrise at the same time. We listen to Everything but the Girl, Jacques Brel, Cesaria Evora, Schubert, opera, all accompanied by a chorus of frogs. Showered and hungry, we glide down the hill for a late dinner.

Today at lunch the sea turns a hazy slate gray. I dig up the old stories. Our years in Holland before children when we were first married. When I had long hair and a beard and wrote a novel in the Royal Library of The Hague. Wendy taught school and we lived in a big, high-ceilinged apartment with a bathtub in the kitchen. We traveled Europe from Norway to Greece. David listens politely. Who knows how many times he has heard them.

Wendy joins in, reminiscing about her first trips to Europe with her family in the early 60s. They followed the Tour de France, saw Charles de Gaulle in Paris, and slept in a brothel in Brussels.

"There was a girl in Brussels..." I say.

"Who liked to sleep in brothels," David says.

"Her father found out."

"And said with a shout."

"Haven't you seen my muscles?"

At Maya's late one night we chat over after-dinner rum with Randy. David, in tie and espadrilles, smokes a cigar. "I still love the smell of a cigar," Randy says. He had to give them up for health reasons. Wendy asks Randy about a man in the restaurant she sees every year. "He's a prominent lawyer. What we call a swamp Yankee."

A well-known English painter is at a nearby table. "I just wrote a review of her show at Gagosian in New York," David says.

"Was it a good review?"

"Yes."

"You should go say hello."

"Not allowed to socialize with the talent."

"Not true."

"What's true is I'm shy."

At La Marine, Isabelle, the *plus petite* of the two *petite* sisters, squats at our table, her head all that is visible. She talks about her newest child. "I had children late. If I had known how much I love being a mother I would have had them earlier."

We order *langouste*. "What size? 500 grams, 600 grams, or 750 grams?"

"One of each," I say.

"500," Wendy says.

"600," David says.

"750," I say. "Small, medium, large. Just like us."

We run into Bernadette in Gustavia and sit down for a drink with her at L'Oubli. "How is Jean-Pierre?"

"He was in a Paris train station when he had the aneurysm. He was on his way back from Kyoto. His vision is not good right now. Otherwise he is O.K."

"When will he come to St. Barts?"

"In early April."

"We're so sorry."

"He was lucky it happened in Paris. He was taken to a hospital immediately and of course doctors there are very good."

"Please give him our love."

"How are you, Bernadette?"

"I had a nightmare," she says softly. "Jean-Pierre was paralyzed."

Colombier beach at the northern end of the island is accessible only by foot or boat. We park the car at the end of Flamands and set off on the rocky trail. It winds through the rugged hillside and counts as serious exercise, especially in the hot sun. It's hard to keep your eye on the bumpy path with the glittering sea at your side. The path rises steeply at times and passes large outcrops of pockmarked volcanic rock. "Are you O.K.?" I ask Wendy. She's afraid of heights.

"Yes, if I don't look down."

The reward is a swim in the sea. That the cove is full of anchored boats doesn't diminish how good the water feels. "Too bad there's not a little bar here," David says.

"Or a rickshaw service."

"Good to go with there is no road."

"Tout à pied."

"Feel like a voyageur."

"I feel like a beer."

"Other end of the line."

A new three-story shopping complex has opened on Quai de la Republique. A depressing mausoleum, it is home to luxury shops, including Tod's and Louis Vuitton. The streets of Gustavia are even more crowded when cruise ships deposit their cargo on shore.

Linen shops in the mall have ironing boards so shopkeepers can iron your newly purchased dress or shirt. Wrinkles come quickly back. Restaurants at night are a field of rumpled cotton. One night the three of us are all wearing linen. "I got this blouse years ago," Wendy says.

"Yes, of course, and so nicely faded."

"I like your new shirt, Dad. Would you say it's mango, or more quince?"

"Quince, I think. Ripe quince."

A complete antithesis to the sterile mall is Fort Karl, a wine shop carved out of rock. "We supply wine to 80 percent of the island's restaurants," Guillaume, the owner says. He's a good-natured, black-haired man who doesn't mind filling up a case or two with decent "good value" wines for individual customers. He leads me into the cave-like recesses of the store where many hundreds of bottles, soldiers of pleasure, lie in wait. Like every good wine merchant, Guillaume likes to help people discover new wines. "Here, try this," he says. "Tell me what you think. *C'est un cadeau.* A gift."

Gustavia in the morning before cars take over is lovely. The air is soft and cool. The shutters of the Creole *casas* are closed. The brightly painted walls of shops and restaurants are fresh and cheering, not garish as they can be at high noon. Fresh and buoyant too are the bougainvillea and palms; they don't, as they can later in the busy blistering day, appear beleaguered.

Mornings (and evenings) you find tan shopkeepers, usually female, standing in doorways, smoking and gossiping. Chestnut-colored gardeners and construction workers in uniforms of shorts, boots, and T-shirts sit outside bakeries and take-away shops. *Le petit dejeuner* is uniform too: croissant, coffee, cigarette.

Gustavia on Sundays when shops are closed and streets are quiet seems more village than sun seeker's mecca. More sleepy, more charming, more of what it was before the onslaught of yachts, fancy stores, and rental Suzukis.

We walk through the port after dinner. The air is heavy, the town lively. Women dance on tables in one bar on Rue du Nord de Mer. At another locals sit outside drinking rum and beer. Music drifts from the cabins of yachts and sailboats. There are more this year. They line almost the entire length of the *quai*, most of them with boarding stairs extended next to baskets of tennis shoes and Top-Siders.

On the boardwalk we pass two French boys flirting with two American girls. One street over on Rue du Genéral de Gaulle, the main drag, all is quiet. Le Select and Bar l'Oubli are boarded up though it's Friday night. The blind man is not out. Two or three islanders sit on a bench enjoying the breeze. Perhaps this is what St. Barts is, a place where a few dance but most go to bed early. A sleepy village with an Hermès store.

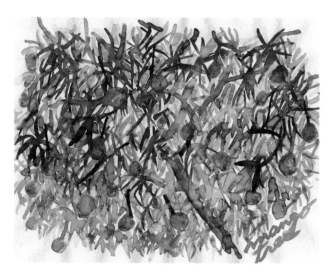

It sounds like popcorn popping. The large tree shoots its seeds—tiny brown-speckled beans—through the air like bullets. The tree has clusters of needled pods, each containing a seed; as they heat up in the hot sun and dry out, they release themselves with a pop and land away from the mother tree. They fly off, one after another. They land on the terrace tiles and burst open. I pick some up and put them on a table. "They're pretty," Wendy says. "Not thinking of starting a collection, are you?"

Wendy is reading *The Epicure's Lament* by Kate Christensen. She reads to me this passage:

> Apropos of something I can't put my finger on, Mary Frances Kennedy Fisher uses the word "plenty" much the same way Hemingway uses the word "good," to conjure up a sense of generous warmth in lean, uncertain times. Sometimes I whisper to myself now... "Serve with plenty of hot buttered toast..." Her "plenty" is a mannered, self-conscious thing, of course, but its repetition, sometimes even stilted overuse, offers a vicarious sense of good American overabundance, stout comfort to those in alien lands and heartsick fugue states alike. "Serve with plenty of hot buttered toast" gives the disaffected and ill-at-ease—me, for example—a momentary welling of joy.

Today is Good Friday. People set up tents on the beach. Families tromp through the sand with baguettes and wine, soccer balls and blankets. It's island tradition to camp out over Easter weekend.

Sundown, the night before *Pâques*, people gather at Shell Beach below the villa to listen to music. Song and chant and throbbing drums echo off the hillside. "Our own private concert," Wendy says. "I love this music." She starts to shimmy.

The sky dissolves into pale washes of blues and pinks then darkens slowly to phthalo blue. Stars, crickets. Sailboats pass in the black sea, lights and masts all that are visible. A large bat circles the pool, once, twice, five times. On each pass it dips elegantly, cleanly into the smooth water.

The pool is like a Turkish bath for neighborhood birds. Sugarbirds bathe from the infinity wall, dipping, shuddering, batting their wings. A pair of vireos hovers, the blue of the water reflected on their breasts, then drop delicately in and out, in and out. Herons and flycatchers sit on the pool's edge like ornaments and drink the chlorinated water.

This morning from the bathroom sink I watch a beautiful *bateau à voile* drift by under sail. The sea on top is a translucent ultramarine dotted with white caps. Below the surface are long sweeps of indigo. A sugarbird dances in the pink trumpet blossoms, a few feet away. A hummingbird flits around. A bathroom without walls means as you enjoy the view mosquitoes enjoy you. And when you take your shower you are joined by a tiny gecko, barely two inches long.

Les financiers are little French cakes similar to *madeleines* but rectangular rather than shell-shaped. Made with brown butter, crushed almonds, and egg whites, they're delicious. We find them at Maya's To Go. Originally made by French nuns in the Middle Ages, *les financiers* became popular in the 19th century when a Parisian baker made them from molds shaped like bars of gold. His bakery was near the Bourse and was frequented by men who worked in the financial district. The cakes are worth their weight in gold.

Easter morning. I walk alone in Gustavia. At the top of a knoll above Shell Beach is where Fort Karl once stood. Here in the 19th century the Swedes kept a few cannons pointed out at the Caribbean. Nearby kids play on a public basketball court that has as a backdrop a nice slice of blue sea.

I walk along Rue de la Colline, high above the town where many permanent residents live. I peer in the window of an appealing antique shop, which I later learn is owned by Sarah's friend Aithana and her husband Jean-Michel. They live above the shop with their two children.

It's pleasant to walk in a local neighborhood far from

the yachting crowd. People putter in gardens, tinker with small boats. The smell of cooking adds to the feeling of quiet domesticity. On the other side of town, above the Catholic church between Rue Gambetta and Rue Victor Hugo, is a lovely old casa, uninhabited and overrun by garden and trees. Removed and private, it has a wonderful view of the harbor.

Up a hill from the house is the former Swedish prison, now a French government office where islanders go to get passports. Built in the 18th century entirely of heavy native stone, it holds its own against hurricanes. The corners are made of black volcanic rock which, difficult to believe, is less brittle and more malleable. The Wall House at the entry to the port, where the town's museum and library are located, is the best example of the way stone buildings were first built on the island. Stones in the early days were laid in rows horizontally, not randomly as they were later. Stone buildings and walls in St. Barts, especially the older ones, are works of art.

Lunch at Randy's and Maya's house. Among those
gathered around a long porch table are the artist Francesco
Clemente, his curly-haired twin sons, Andrea and Pietro,
Bill Katz, the designer and architect, and his young lover
Brian. Francesco and I flank Maya, Wendy sits between
Francesco and Randy.

Francesco's face is familiar from his self-portraits. His
close cropped hair has turned salt and pepper as has his
beard. Vying for attention with his pale piercing eyes are
drop amethyst earrings. Not tall but with great presence,
he has a thick Italian accent (he is from Naples) and a wry
bemused charm.

Bill Katz is tall and thin and dressed in flowing plaid
silk trousers. Gracious and appealing, he has short hair
and a tan handsome face. We talk about the opening of

a new museum in Naples where a room will be devoted
to Clemente's work. "The museum is actually old but is
reopening as a new museum," Clemente says.

"We're going to the opening," Randy says. "We're
also going to the opening of a restaurant in Alba that Bill
designed.

"Food and art. What could be better?"

"In Italy!" Wendy says.

A longtime set and costume designer, Bill is now in
demand as a designer of houses and restaurants. He designed
the restaurant Chanterelle in New York and is currently
working on an apartment for Anselm Kiefer in Paris.

Food is served on big platters. Salads of cucumber and
mint, mango and tomato. Brandade, lentils, and plantain.
Stories are told, bottles of rosé consumed, and, in the end,
after a soft rain falls on the hills and in the valley, Maya
brings out a fruit tart that looks like a painting.

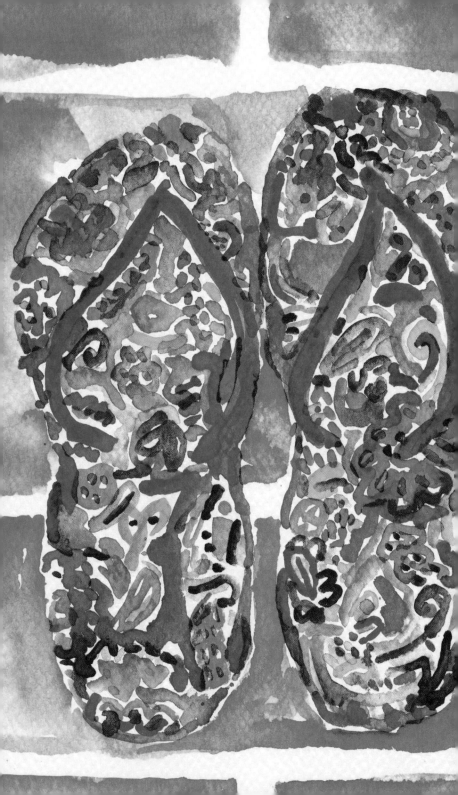

TEN

La tempête, la tempête, everybody is talking about *la tempête.*

The hurricane-like storm rages for days. Streets and beaches are flooded, boardwalks buckled, concrete planters overturned. Boats flee Gustavia for safer harbors. *"La tempête est très forte,"* Rose, the housekeeper, says. "More like September."

It moves on finally but leaves us unsettled. The sun is out, the wind less marauding. Still the waves at Gouverneur toss us around. "I don't like getting thwonked," Wendy says.

"Imagine a real hurricane."

The yacht in the cove glows in the black sea. Crickets whine in the breeze, bats, fast and silent, skim the surface of the pool. The Moroccan lights are on. There is rumba music. Our bodies still feel the heat of the sun. We hear French voices from a nearby house, the sound of forks on plates. We are about to have dinner. Down the hill in a restaurant by the harbor, if we can pull ourselves away.

"Men can read Jane Austen," David says. He's reading *Emma,* who, with her tendency to foster romantic relationships and frequent bouts of mortification, reminds him of his mother.

Books are devoured. Sarah finds *The Brief Wondrous Life of Oscar Wao* by Junot Díaz riveting, if disturbing. "I don't want our family to have the curse of 'fukú.'" Wendy, prime devourer, polishes off *Butterball*, a collection of short stories by Maupassant, *Mister Pip* by the New Zealand writer Lloyd Jones, and *A World of Love* by Elizabeth Bowen. Also *Claudine's House*, Colette's childhood memoir.

I read *Life Class*, Pat Barker's book about English artists and World War I.

"Another cheerful book, Dad?" Sarah says.

"Not exactly. It's the act of reading that's important. If the writing is good, it buoys you up, the book keeps you from sinking."

"Like a life preserver," Sarah says.

"Exactly. A good book is a life preserver."

Lines from Barker's *Life Class*:

Nighttime was best. London in the dark still had an excitement, a glamour, that it had entirely lost by day. The cold and gloom made the Café Royal seem fragile, a bubble floating on a black river. At first he thought nothing had changed, but then he looked again more closely and realized everything had.

Burnt-butter smears of khaki darkened the red and gold.
Young men everywhere: carefully cultivated mustaches over
mouths not yet thinned into certainty, breeches and puttees
self-consciously worn. Out there, the war stank of blood and
gangrene; here, it smelled of new clothes.

The Bucket is the annual get-together of 30 100-foot
sailboats that race gracefully if competitively around the
island. Most are modern technological wonders, but a few
have wooden decks and masts and elaborate arrangements of
old-fashioned sails.

The boats pass below the villa close enough for us
to hear the shuddering of unfurling sails and to see large
crews in matching shirts massed together. The giant sails are
triangles of white and gray and cream layered against the
blue. Dark hulls lean into the white caps. It's a spectacle of
geometry and dance.

"More enjoyable to look at a sailboat," I say, "than to be
tossed about on one."

"Bien sur," Sarah says. *"Je n'aime pas le mal de mer."* She lifts a
glass of wine to the sea.

"The sails are called laundry," Wendy says. "I read it in a
magazine."

"Sheets in the wind," David says.

Island roads thicken in spring with cars full of chilled
humans seeking sun. Scores of Terios, Suzukis, and Mini
Coopers along with Mokes and *motos* bounce back and forth
like pinballs between Gustavia and St. Jean, up and down the
hills of Colombier and Lurin, to and from the beaches.

On our way to dinner, we are caught in a long net of
cars curling out of Gustavia. An approaching car stops to let
us through a gap on Rue de la Republique. "I don't think we

can make it."

"You're right about that," the driver of the stopped car says through the open window. He is next to me on the left. We manage to slip through and continue around the harbor.

"That was David Letterman," Sarah says.

"I thought his voice sounded familiar."

"King of sarcasm," David says.

"Well, he was a good Samaritan then," Wendy says.

Easing down the driveway into the peaceful confines of the villa, you forget about busy roads. The green hill rolling down to blue water is tonic, the steady horizon an instant balm. Beauty is often in the margins. You have to work to find it. Go out of your way for its blessing.

After a brief shower, a rainbow spreads across the sky, intensely vivid, each end of the arc dancing on the sea. A giant moth settles on the wall in the dining room. It stays unmoving for hours. Fragile, haunting, with patterned wings of rich gray, blue, and brown, it is a living painting.

Iguana! On the terrace big and fierce-looking with a satanic grin. Electric green scales, back of arrowheads, long tail like a whip. It climbs up on a wall. It doesn't look shy and harmless, seeking pieces of banana or hibiscus blossoms. It pauses for a moment, aware, it seems, that we are transfixed by its strange prehistoric shape, the power of its otherness. It disappears calmly into the brush.

"They're endangered in South America," I say. "People eat them."

The dark hummingbird, neon crest aglow, keeps me company as I brush my teeth. It's there every morning as if expecting me. What is the connection between these creatures and us? I think of Verdine the iguana treading regularly through Jean-Pierre's house. She comes when called, but does she come only for food or for something else?

Do the doves know me or know only the bread crumbs I spread on the tiles? I talk to them, I call to them (my coo

is pretty good). Over time I could probably feed them by hand. I would name them, pet them. We humans are animals. We bond not just with dogs and cats but with animals in the wild. It's a bond beyond the sharing of food. It's a deep affinity, a line that runs between spirits, spirits with wings or spirits with hands.

David is never far from book or laptop, or from making a witty remark. He puts on his goggles and swims his morning laps. He studies the dinner menu. With his princely manners (his long hair is pulled back over his ears)

and amusing stories, he is good company. He is writing a feature article for *Art in America* on Phillip Taaffe.

We talk about the presidential campaign. Hillary, Barack, John McCain. We talk about movies, architecture, art, books, restaurants. And sports. "How can curling be on ESPN rather than soccer?" He likes the walk along the harbor after dinner. "Cigars and stars."

Sarah is out every night after dinner and often all night, somewhat to my chagrin. She may be 30, but when she is under our roof (even a rented roof), I become the protective father. Too protective, she says. The villa phone rings. Her island friends want her to come out and play. Fun-loving and funny, passionate and compassionate, she lights up a room. Dressed up or down she's always stylish.

There are tears and sadness. "Bobby the pirate died," she tells us. And she is distressed over a close friend's illness. Sarah lives in Los Angeles where she works as a costumer and stylist for television and film. She decides to stay a few more days on the island. "Tell me the names of people you know," I say.

"There's Marco the hairdresser, Alejandro the Brazilian waiter and former model, Bertrand the yacht owner, Nicolas the chef, Thierry the owner of La Plage, Sophie the mother

of Sam and Fiona, Max the journalist, the waiters Franc *un* and Franc *deux*. Then there's…"

Late morning in Gustavia, we run into Jean-Pierre on Rue Jeanne d'Arc. We go to La Bête à Zailes for a beer. "I walk an hour a day. Doctor's orders. I have to get out of the house."

He seems more robust than last year, more recovered from his stroke. The twinkle in his eye is back and his raffish charm surfaces quickly. He lights a cigarette. "I won't stop smoking. No meat, no salt, so sugar, the doctors say. I would rather live a shorter life with my pleasures than a longer boring life." We talk of cold, gray Paris, beautiful, expensive St. Barts. His hair is bright white still, the tattoo on his tan forearm still catches the eye. "I cannot paint. My eyes are not good."

He sips his beer. "I went to Africa last year. I have to feel I am still alive. I went with a friend. We hired a guide and a cook on the Internet. We took a canoe down the Niger in Mali. The Sahara is on one side, savannah on the other."

"How was the food?"

"We ate goat and a lot of chicken. *Poulets de la bicyclette.* Chickens with long, skinny legs that run so fast there is no meat on them."

They traveled through Dogon country, they rode camels, drove four-wheelers, admired the turbans of the Tuareg. "I went to Timbuktu. It has always been a place of magic in my mind." His phone rings. "It's Bernadette. Time for lunch. I have to go. *À bientôt.*" He hugs Wendy, shakes my hand. "So good to see you."

"So good to see you, Jean-Pierre. Love to Bernadette. Take care."

"They don't make them like that anymore," Wendy says as he walks away.

"Beaches his sailboat on an island and never leaves."

I go for a walk in town. In backstreet yards bright allamanda and hibiscus spill over broken-down jet skis, rusty barbecues, and collapsing jungle gyms. Cats slip through slotted fences, dogs look up from slumber. A boy in droopy jeans and cocked baseball cap carries a branch of bright bananas. A tan girl in a short skirt steers her scooter neatly around a corner. Old Range Rovers are bunched up outside a garage like cattle in rain.

In the *papeterie* on Rue Jeanne d'Arc I buy ink, heavy
cotton paper, and old-style French portfolios. I check out
an exhibit of black-and-white island photographs in the big
stone museum. Near the end of the harbor is the new town
hall with its garish row of ballooning white columns. France's
timeworn motto—*liberté, egalité, fraternité*—spreads across the
building's high gable. Above it is the island's coat of arms: a
shield propped up by the webbed feet of two pelicans. Long
part of a commune under Guadeloupe's jurisdiction, the
people of St. Barts recently voted to become a self-governing
collectivité of France.

Sailboats line up along the dock in front of city hall.
Dinghies run to and from boats moored in the outer harbor.
On one crowded rubber boat a large Golden Retriever stands
up front, tall and proud, looking like a masthead. Walking
back up the hill to the villa, I stop during a rain shower under
a spray of bougainvillea and look down on the pretty town
wrapped around its harbor.

Wendy and I hike on a high bluff that juts out into the
Atlantic. Steep in places, its views of ocean and rocky cliffs
are spectacular. Not even goats accompany us, though clearly
this is their terrain. We are alone with the wind, the rock
sculptures and spiky cactus, the unending blue.

Looking back, we see charred fields and blackened stone
walls, the result of a fire set by an arsonist a few days ago.
"Unbelievable someone would do that."

"Paradise in smoke."

A last dinner at Maya's. Randy and Maya sit down at
our table at the end of the evening. "I heard Jack's on the
island," Sarah says.

"Jack Benny?" Randy says. "No, he's dead. Not Jack Nicklaus. No golf."

"Jack Jack."

"He was here in the restaurant last night."

"Avec son entourage," Maya says.

"Oh that Jack."

"That Jack."

Talk turns from celebrities to fashion to food to getting kicked out of boarding school. As we leave, amid hugs and kisses and *à la prochaines,* Maya hands Wendy a big bottle of the house-made shrub. "For you," she says. "To drink at home. *Chez vous.*"

"Only after dinner," Randy says. "Or Sunday after church."

"Can we get it back safely?" I ask.

"Don't worry, she'll find a way," Sarah says.

ELEVEN

Luxury is an outdoor shower, especially at night.

Stars, the moon, lights on a distant island flickering across the sea. The soap, a big creamy bar, smells of vanilla. The water is hot and surprisingly strong, the breeze mild. Crickets chirp, a bird warbles. On the wall is a gecko, glutinous with black bulging eyes, fixed as if in a herpetologist's box.

"What time is dinner?"

"Eight-thirty. Same as always."

Much of life here is given over to the body. Carnal pleasure yes, but more to simple stimulation of the senses: sun bathing, massage, exercise, dress, jewelry. Not to mention epicurean delights—voluptuous mango, tender *langouste*, old rum. Decadence? No, enjoyment plain and simple.

Churchill once wrote to his brother: "We live very simply—but with all the essentials of life well understood and well provided for—hot baths, cold Champagne, new peas and old brandy." A good epitaph.

The bright white hacienda-like villa spreads across the hill behind a long railing of balustrades. Built in 1960, it's light-filled and, if now a little rough around the edges, has a

lot of character. We love the setting, both wild and quiet. It
faces a broad canvas of sea painted in a variety of blues by
Homer or Monet, take your pick. Clouds swim in the sky,
snatches of white cotton, scrims of Tiepolo pink when the
sun sets, piles of rain laden gray. The islands of Nevis and
St. Eustache (and occasionally St. Kitts) are pale phantasms
on clear days. A few houses dot the surrounding hillsides of
cactus and windblown trees. The hills drop precipitously into
the lapping sea. We hear the waves. Gouverneur beach is a
seven-minute walk down a steep road.

Like the Durrels in Corfu, we commingle with nature.
Doves fly through the house, kingbirds dip in the pool.
Humpback whales spout and splash in the distant blue.
Tortoises peer at us from the garden ledge. They eat fallen
flowers but prefer mango and banana. They pull at bits of
food in our hands with their beaks, push at rinds with their
inverted legs.

This year there are five. They have proliferated on the island over the years and now drivers stop often to carry them across the road.

Goats traipse freely up and down the hills, roosters and hens peck in the dirt under the ficus trees. One morning I had to crawl up the cactus-thick hillside to free a crying baby goat whose leg was trapped beneath a branch.

There is a gazebo on the other side of the pool where I go to draw, and Wendy and Sarah to read out of the sun. David sits at the long wooden table on the terrace staring above his open laptop at the beautiful view.

David is here for two weeks. He's vacationing and working on a book, his second. His first, *Men and Style*, was published last fall. He figures he's earned extra time on the island and that the blue sea and bright sun will be inspiring. Sarah, taking a break from her busy life as fashion stylist and designer, is also here for two weeks. They've joined Wendy and me almost every year we've been here—over 20 now.

I open my tin of watercolors under the gazebo. As if on cue, the dove flutters to the tiles, its wings whistling. It bobs its head and looks at me with a dark liquid eye. I have a scrap of bread in my bag. It scurries around and pecks at the crumbs.

The sun catches the dove's colors: iridescent mauve, dusty apricot, gray brown. *La tourterelle* (as it's called on the island) seems made to be held in your hand. Its head and breast have a perfect roundness. White doves flew freely in Matisse's studio. He held them as he sketched. Soft, gentle, shy, the dove, like peace, is an improbable thing.

"Fabio made this for you." Yasmine hands Wendy a jar. "It's marmalade made from villa oranges."

"How nice. Thank you."

Yasmine is the villa caretaker. A vibrant, pretty woman, she was born on Martinique to a Greek father and French mother. After 15 years in Guadeloupe, they moved to St. Barts where her father became the island's first surveyor. Fabio is her Italian husband and father of their three daughters.

Every morning when Yasmine comes to the house she chats with us, telling stories in a delightful accent about the island or her family. "We go to the U.S. on holiday. To the parks and the mountains. To Colorado and California. We travel by RV. They are wonderful. Everything is in one place, the kitchen, the bathroom, the bed. Small and it goes with you. I love RV."

The shell museum in Corossol is closed. "It's always
closed when we're here."

"I love the sign," David says.

I remember the time years ago when it was open. Thousands of shells everywhere presided over by a rather crusty man who seemed to have spent much of his life on the seven seas. It was not scientific or organized in any particular way. It was more like a personal collection, and more interesting for that. As the collection grew and the collector aged, he decided to open a "museum" and charge admission. At least that's one theory. Now perhaps he is too old to run it.

The fishing village of Corossol has the flavor of old St. Barts. Creole houses inhabited for generations by native islanders line the narrow main street. Most of the clapboard or shingled houses are in need of paint and repair, but they still have the original architecture. They have their old Creole porches and balconies and carved fanciful trim.

Faded pastel facades are barely visible behind gardens of tangled vines and flowers, lush palms and mango trees. Several houses are empty and decaying. "It feels like a real neighborhood," Wendy says.

The village road runs down to a beach. The sea so near must provide relief from small rooms. The sea, and the TVs and radios, you hear through open windows. Dinghies and small fishing boats are tied to a dock. *Langouste* traps and coils of rope are piled on the landing. A few people sunbathe on the narrow strip of sand. There is a large rock with a cross dedicated to islanders lost at sea.

The squall builds quickly in the blue sky. "Is it coming our way?" It's hard to tell if the curtain of rain will pass over us or beyond us. We scramble to close doors and the gazebo studio. It starts gently then pounds the villa's metal roof. Water splashes in, the dove lingers in the doorway. Then. . .it's gone, leaving in its wake freshness not only in the air but in us. Also, oddly, the smell of earth.

The island is very dark at night, as is any place removed from city lights. The depth of the darkness may be disconcerting at first but over time, as you come to know it, it's a source of wonder. Sometimes, returning from dinner, I turn off the car lights when we round the corner above Gouverneur. It's scary, shocking, and magical all at the same time. The hills backlit by the moon are dark silhouettes, the sea a rippling pewter gray.

We lay back on the terrace chairs and look up at the indigo sky covered in white dots, like a fancy silk dress. "What's that wonderful smell?"

"Lilies blooming."

We fall asleep, intoxicated by the heavy perfume.

Drinks one evening with Ben and Becky, friends from home.

"How long have you been coming?" Wendy asks.

"Twenty-five years."

"When we first came, part of the road on Lurin wasn't paved."

Near the terrace is a camera on a tripod with a large telephoto lens. It's pointed at the pond below the villa. A bulldozer is parked by the pond.

"What will happen to the pelicans when the pond is gone?"

"Have to find new feeding grounds." Becky is a wildlife photographer, mostly of birds. She has published several books of her work, including books on the birds of St. Barts and neighboring islands.

"Not that many different kinds of birds on the island," I say.

"More than you think," Becky says.

"I've seen pelicans, egrets, hummingbirds, frigatebirds."

"Doves, sugarbirds. The parrot at Le Tamarin."

"Have you seen the gray king bird? How about the brown booby?"

"Ben, do you go with Becky when she takes pictures?"

"No. I stay here and read."

"He plays *boules.*"

"Really? With the locals."

"Yes."

"Do you have your own *boule?*"

   Yasmine arrives today with a small box. "I found it in my garden." Inside, surrounded by leaves of lettuce, is a fully formed and alert baby tortoise, maybe five inches long. "I will let it go on the hillside. Safer here than by my house."

   "Can you tell if it's male or female?" Sarah asks.

   "Yes, when they are adults. You turn them over. The female's stomach is flat, the male's is..." She makes a scooping motion with her her hand. "So he can climb on top. All they do is eat and make babies. We hear them."

   "They make a noise? Their shells rubbing together?"

   "No, they make sounds with their voices."

"Turtles have voices?"

"They hiss, don't they?"

We go to the garden. Yasmine picks up one of the big ones. "This one is male, you can see." She picks up another. "Female."

"We haven't heard any tortoises…"

"Clucking. That's the sound they make. Clucking or grunting."

"I have to adjust," Jean-Marc says. "The island is changing. Everything is so expensive. Even the prices on my menu." We sit at his restaurant a few feet from the water. Masts of sailboats sway like trees on a lakeshore. Inside La Bête à Zailes, a band from New York, plays a Fleetwood Mac song.

"When did you open the restaurant?"

"Eighteen years ago. Don't you think the island has changed?"

"Yes and no. It's still nice."

"Too much bling-bling. Too corporate. It's hard for a local restaurant like mine."

The young waiter places a platter of fish on our table.

His name is Daniel. He's from Budapest. "I've been here seven months."

"Are there any other Hungarians on the island?"

"I've met three so far."

"Do you like it here?"

"Oh, yes. It's so pure."

A good book counts for a lot, both when you're reading it and when you think about reading it. To me, it's one of life's necessities. To bury your head page after page, chapter after chapter, is to be lost to time, to find yourself in another world.

"Finished."

"Did you read that in one day?"

"I finished mine in three."

"Did you read every page?"

"I think I've read all the books we brought."

"What are you going to do now?"

Trouble in paradise. Gouverneur beach is covered with sargassum. Strong currents sweep the brown seaweed into the waters around the island and onto the beaches. Piles of the bubble-like kelp collect on the sand and only hardcore vacationers spread towels. "I saw it from the villa floating around."

"It smells if they don't clean it up."

"Getting worse in the Caribbean. Global warming, no doubt."

"Isn't it normal?"

"Yes, they named the Sargasso Sea after it. I think it lives or forms in coral reefs.

But warmer water probably makes it grow more."

"I always thought Sargasso Sea was a romantic name."

"Wonder how long it will last?"

"Well, I'm going for a swim."

I paddle through the clumps of seaweed. I look back at Wendy and Sarah huddled on the beach under the gray sky. Farther out it's not so bad and I can swim normally.

"It's a country rat," Yasmine says. "It's not as bad as a city rat."

"Really?"

"Just as ugly."

"It nibbled on the melons."

Sarah came upon the creature in the kitchen last night after we had closed up the house for bed. She ran into our bedroom screeching. Yasmine calls Fabio who appears on his motorcycle and fiddles with a device that emits a high-pitched noise rats don't like. It doesn't work.

Tonight when I go into the kitchen, I see the long black tail disappear behind the garbage bin. "Just pretend it's *The Nutcracker.* Wendy and Sarah are not amused.

I stand over the long wooden table on the terrace looking out at the sea. The wind blows the sheet of paper I'm brushing with watercolor. "Do you think Turner ever wore a sarong? Or Cézanne. They were watercolorists."

"Hockney probably has."

Today on the beach we meet a French woman named Lolo. Mosaic artist and private chef, she has lived on the island for 35 years. "It's not always a vacation," she says. "I have to work hard." Towel in hand, she points in the direction of the water. "The waves are strong. There is an undertow. Be careful."

Wendy stays back as I march to the shore. A giant wave immediately knocks me down. I roll in the turf as the waves push me around. I feel hands.

"Are you all right?" A man tries to lift me up.

"Yes, I'm fine. Thank you."

Wendy and Lolo come down to the water.

"*Ça va?*" Lolo says.

"*Oui. Un peu embarrassé.*" I wade back into the water, sand in my ears, nose, swimsuit.

Pride goeth before the sea.

A last dinner at Maya's. "We're sitting at the same table we sat at the first time we came to the island."

"Creatures of habit."

"Creatures of pleasure."

"I still love it."

"More houses, more cars, more cruise ships."

"More rats."

"More fancy stores."

"So you don't like it anymore?"

"Let's toast to what we do like."

"Tortoises."

"Orange pound cake."

"Cuban cigars."

"Jane Austen."

"Tamarind trees."

"Friends."

"Rum."

"Mango and tomato salad."

"Sugarbirds."

"View from Villa Lassus."

"Children in their little sailboats."

"The moon that smiles."

"Breeze."

"The blue."

Nothing is better than walking to the beach. No car, no phone, no book, only a towel and a cap. I am faster than a turtle, slower than a hummingbird, which becomes empirically clear as I stride down the hill. This a new habit. In the early days, the beach at Gouverneur was too far to walk. The idea of walking rather than driving to get some place seems positively quaint. You get some exercise, of course, but you also get life up close, see unfiltered more of what's out there. You feel and learn more on foot. Especially when you're in the natural world.

I like the ritual. The view of the sea as I round the curve, the tall coconut palms at the edge of the estate that borders the beach, the red of the oleander blossoms, the beehives, even the smell of the chicken coop. The view at the curve is Edenic, as pure as the background of a Renaissance painting. A wedge of sea and clouds framed by rocky hills and a spread of lush green trees. Descendants of Adam and Eve are nowhere about.

Today when I hike down I find a bird's nest in a thorn bush. When I look closer, a sugarbird scoots out. Passing under the low branches of the tree guarding the beach and stepping onto the sand is somehow momentous. It's an occasion, fresh each time.

The walk back up is something else. I pause for a moment to catch my breath. I look out at the holy sea and the heavenly sky coming down to meet it.

Blue

NOTE: *This book was finished before Hurricane Irma swept through the Caribbean in the fall of 2017, leaving many islands in shambles, including St. Barts. It was the worst storm ever to hit the island. The people of St. Barts are working, with spirit and determination, to rebuild their lives and to restore the beauty of their island home.*

ACKNOWLEDGMENTS

I want to thank powerHouse Books for bringing *Blue* to life. Wes Del Val and Krzysztof Poluchowicz, it was a pleasure to work with you again. I'm grateful to Lizzi Sandell, who edited the book. I would also like to thank Megan Wilson who kindly permitted the design scheme she created for the cover of *Paris in Winter* (published by powerHouse Books in 2015) to be used for *Blue*.

Many thanks to the people of St. Barts for their vibrant spirit and love of life. To Randy and Maya, special thanks for your generous and witty friendship, the many terrific meals, and for taking Sarah under your wing a time or two. To Jean-Pierre and Bernadette, *mille mercis* for the evenings of wine and laughter, for your kindness and warmth. To Ana and Yves, Yasmine and Fabio, thanks for making life on the beautiful island even more beautiful.

Big hugs to the many friends, old and new, from home and abroad, that we shared time with on the island. It was a pleasure and a privilege.

As always infinite love and gratitude to Wendy, David, and Sarah. Some of the best hours of our lives were spent together on this small island in the French West Indies. To those hours, to those memories, to you, I say, *"Chacha la vie!"*

Blue

A ST. BARTS MEMOIR

―――――――――

Text and images © 2018 David Coggins

All rights reserved. No part of this book may be reproduced in
any manner in any media, or transmitted by any means whatsoever,
electronic or mechanical (including photocopy, film or video recording,
Internet posting, or any other information storage and retrieval
system), without the prior written permission of the publisher.

Published in the United States by powerHouse Books,
a division of powerHouse Cultural Entertainment, Inc.
37 Main Street, Brooklyn, NY 11201-1021
e-mail: info@powerHouseBooks.com
website: www.powerHouseBooks.com

First edition, 2018

Library of Congress Control Number: TKTK

ISBN 978-157687-897-2

Printing and binding by Pimlico Book International

Book design by Krzysztof Poluchowicz (powerHouse Books)
and David Coggins

Type is set in Centaur, originally drawn by Bruce Rogers in 1914 for
the Metropolitan Museum of Art.

10 9 8 7 6 5 4 3 2 1

Printed and bound in China

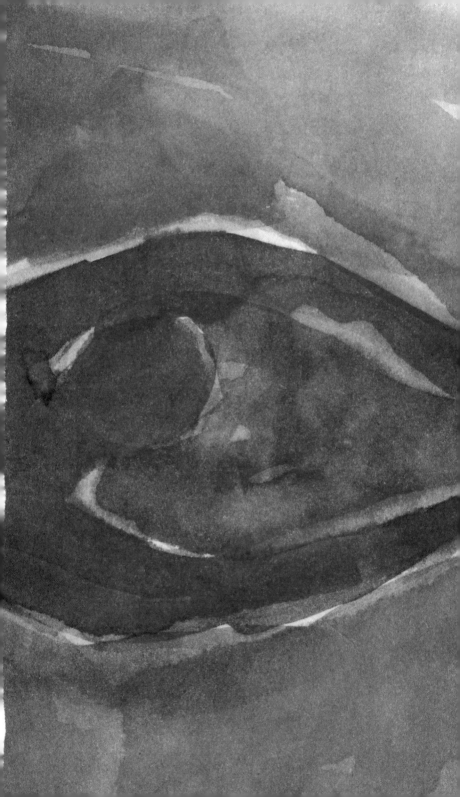